In Praise of *Hug Me Anyway*

"As a musician, these poems strike me as a symphony of emotions—from the mournful hum of an elegy to the lively beat of satire, from quiet reflection to joyous celebration. They share a common thread: a voice that's genuine, heartfelt, and unassuming, with a sharp ear for the rhythm and melody of words. Whether you're grieving, laughing, or marching with the crowd, this collection is there, meeting you where you are—with soul, resilience, and a pen that knows how to hit all the right notes."

Danny O'Flaherty,
international Celtic Balladeer, musician, and songwriter.

"Barbara Sillery brilliantly puts the language through the paces displaying pathos, humor, and lots of thoughtfulness . . . word play at its finest in "Gone" when Sillery ponders the words for "death." If it is possible for there to be verbal mortar shells, one poem had me temporarily stunned. Entitled "I Didn't Ask", the poem is a granddaughter's lament about conversations she regrets not having had with her immigrant grandparents. The emotional impact is best experienced alone. Fortunately, there is the rest of the book for all of us to share."

Errol Laborde, When Rex Met Zulu:
And Other Chronicles of the New Orleans Experience.

"From award-winning documentarian and writer Barbara Sillery comes *Hug Me Anyway*—A striking, off beat and, at times, bad ass collection of poetry and photographs that takes us into the world of witches and warlocks, ghosts, and even Chicken Little. Sillery's love of language and her background loom large throughout this collection that reflects her experience living in New England and NOLA. Just how good is the language? Check out *Big Girl Panties* or *Que*. Or the lament of a falling sky, the salvation of nature's heart hugs in *Ghosts Within*. *Gone* takes a tongue-in-cheek look at clichés describing death—"kick the bucket" and "bought the farm" and, in which Bugs Bunny and Sillery remind us, "That's All Folks!"

Donna Harrison,
Sandwich Arts Alliance, Literary Arts

Hug Me Anyway

Barbara Sillery

Cover photo: Patrick Eul

Cover design: Patrick Eul and Lucy Arnold

All photos are by the author except where noted.

ISBN 978-1-950251-18-6 (paperback)

Library of Congress Control Number: 2025909781

First edition

Printed in the United States of America

Published by The National League of American Pen Women, Inc.

PEN WOMEN PRESS

Founded in 1897, the National League of American Pen Women, Inc. is a nonprofit dedicated to promoting the arts.

NLAPW, Inc. 1300 17th Street NW,

Washington, D.C. 20036-1973; www.nlapw.org

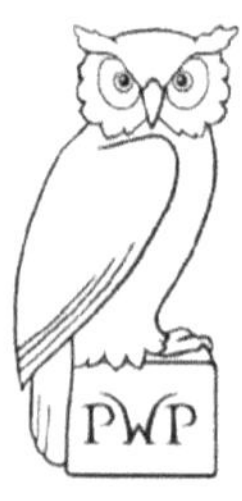

To Danielle, Rebecca, Heather
Michael and Leila

You are my heart.

Books by Barbara Sillery

The Haunting of Louisiana

The Haunting of Mississippi

Biloxi Memories

The Haunting of Cape Cod and the Islands

Haunted Cape Cod

Haunted Louisiana

*Haunted Cape Cod's Sea Captains, Shipwrecks,
and Spirits*

Haunted Mississippi Delta and Beyond

Haunted Nantucket

Contents

In Praise of *Hug Me Anyway* i

Books by Barbara Sillery vii

Intro to my Ramblings x

Apology In D Minor 1

Big Girl Panties 3

Hoops and Hurdles 5

Who's On First 7

Giggles and Groans 11

Trust 13

Close Apart 15

File: Baby Lost 19

Fairy Wood Nymph 21

The Gift 23

Swim Mate 25

Diane 27

Older Than 31

La Nouvelle Orléans 33

Carnival Time 35

Random Thoughts from the Bayou 37

Witches Brew 39

Magic 41

The Necessary 43

This Pen 45

Signs To Ponder 47

Victory 53

Walkin' 55

Sir Elton Non 57

Time Later 59

Killing Time 61

Que 63

Not Today 65

Attack of the Uglies 67

Fixin' to 69

Another One Down 71

Man with Suit & Tie 73

Gone 75

Kiss My Grits 79

The Old Ways Live 81

I Didn't Ask 83

Ghosts Within 85

Loving Myself 87

Thank you, Sir James M. Barrie 89

—DO THAT 91

Acknowledgements 93

About the Author 95

Intro to my Ramblings

Eons ago, I was privileged to be a part of a theatre troupe that performed Edgar Lee Master's poignant play *Spoon River Anthology*. The characters speak in free verse, monologues interspersed with heart rendering songs. The lyrics to the song *I am I am* continue to resonate with me: "We're bound together, this world and me, I am a part of the things I see. I am of nature, it is of me … I am I am." In that sense, the poems contained within these pages are autobiographical. Some are more personal than others. Some are fragments, fleeting emotions, thoughts. All are meant to tell a story.

The title poem *Apology in D Minor* is a journey I'm still on, but now at least, I have a glimmer of where I am going. While working on the documentary *From the Wake of the Bow* for a New Orleans PBS station, the crew and I were in Bayou Lafourche, South Louisiana. As the producer, I interviewed a master boat builder in the bowels of his hand-made (no design plans), thirty-two-foot wooden trawler (shrimp boat). Melvin Kiff was proudly pointing to the ribs inside the hull, "See how close apart they are." My novice eyes and even more bewildered brain tried to come to terms with the unfamiliar construction concept. "Close-apart" is a phrase that now has a treasured place in my lexicon where I will forever cherish the rolling Cajun French cadence and wisdom of Melvin Kiff.

Swim Mate pokes gentle fun at my oldest daughter's grueling days as a competitive swimmer with United States Swimming. All three of my daughters shared an ever-growing menagerie of pets: cats, ferrets, gerbils, fish, horses, a dog, a rabbit, an iguana, and even a ball python. Somehow when they left for college, I became the primary caretaker. *Walkin'* is the tale of my daily ritual with my middle daughter's cat, Dawg, and my youngest child's dog, Sam.

One Christmas, my youngest, who we called Tinkerbell, insisted on sleeping under the Christmas tree. *The Gift* percolated from that night. *La Nouvelle Orléans* and *Carnival* are my tributes to a city that continues to inspire.

I Didn't Ask is a belated acknowledgement of my Ukrainian heritage; on my maternal side I am half Ukrainian. My father and his mother-in-law had a loving relationship. But my father, a perennial tease, would periodically get a rise out of my grandmother's normally reticent personality by questioning if she was Russian. My tiny four-foot-something-ish grandmother would respond in an explosion of words, proudly declaring she was Ukrainian. The torrent of anger would subside over a shared bowl of homemade pea soup.

Falling in and out of love is magic fused with heartache. *Loving Myself, Fixin' to, Attack of the Uglies* are questions and pitfalls we face everyday; it's the getting back up that counts. *Another One Down, Older Than, Man with Suit and Tie,* and *Gone* reflect my obsession with death and its effect on the living. *Ghosts Within* honors the cultural documentaries I have produced and the books I have written during my career.

Read into these poems whatever you need.

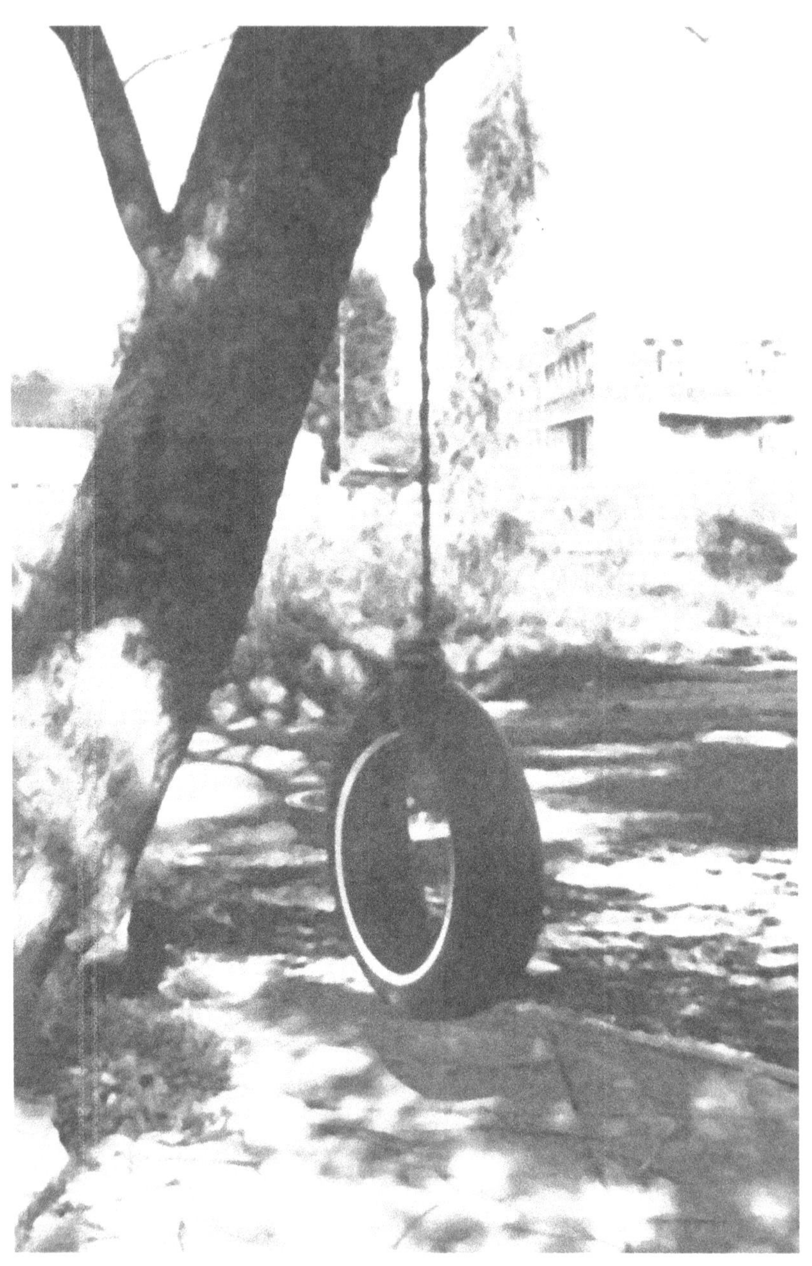

Apology in D Minor
Photo by Danielle Genter

Apology In D Minor

The sky is falling.
There's a hole in the ground.
Hug me. Hug me, now.

The road is too narrow.
The hill is too steep.
Hug me, hug me quick.

I didn't do it right.
I didn't do it at all.
Hug me. Hold me. Please.

It just happened, that's all. It
does you know—flat tires, gray
hairs, wrong turns, hurricanes,
fires, floods, pestilence, and
then there's that big one—*Woe.*
A half a hug would do.

It sounds better in French:
Je ne sâis pas pourquoi—
I do not know why, but
the logic remains as pitiful.
So, perhaps, *s'il vous plaît,*
un petite hug pour moi?

So, here I stand awaiting
the verdict, wishing I could
create a reason, even an
unreason would be nice.
But what if there isn't?
Hug me anyway?

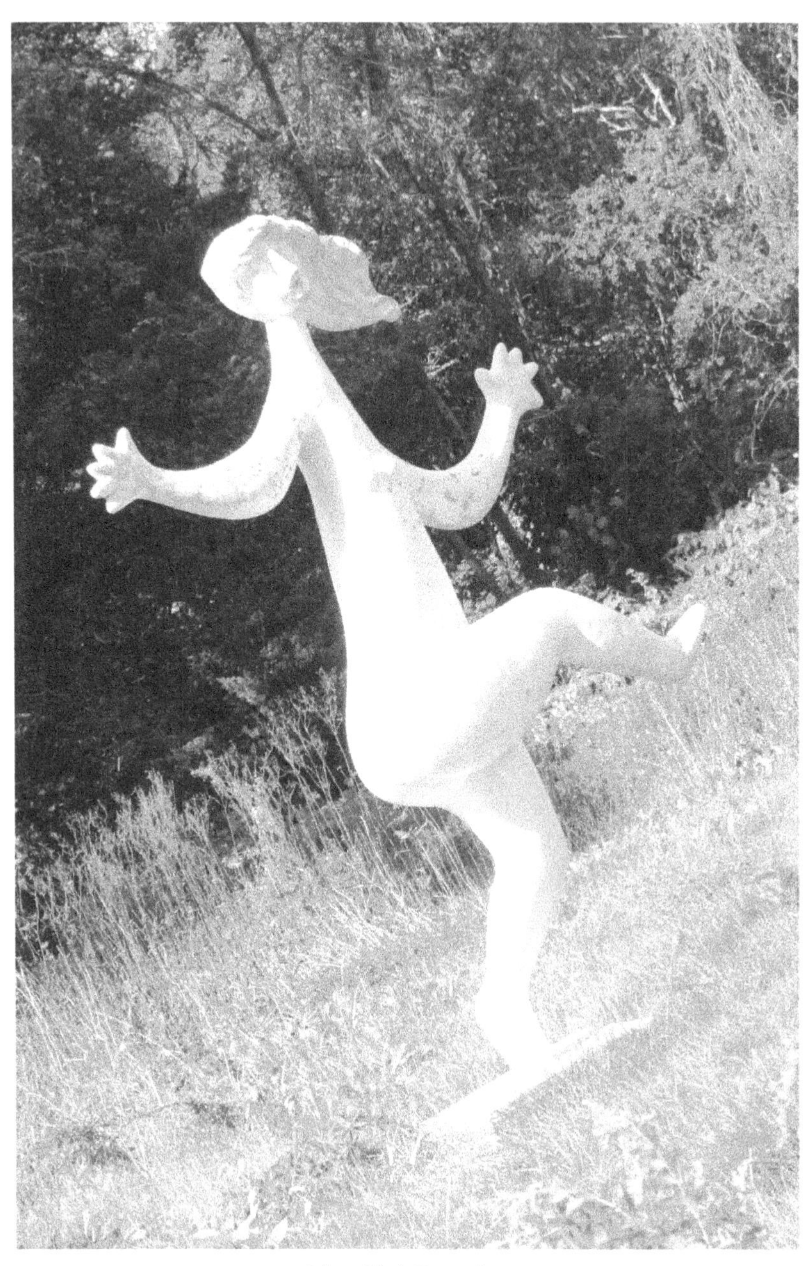

Big Girl Panties
Sculptor Thomas Maley. Bad Martha Brewery,
Falmouth, MA.

Big Girl Panties

Lost:
Big Girl Panties.
If found return to
bawling woman
in closet.

Fair Warning:
If unrecoverable,
naked woman may
roam the streets.

Said woman
non-aggressive,
non-verbal,
in need of
a hug.

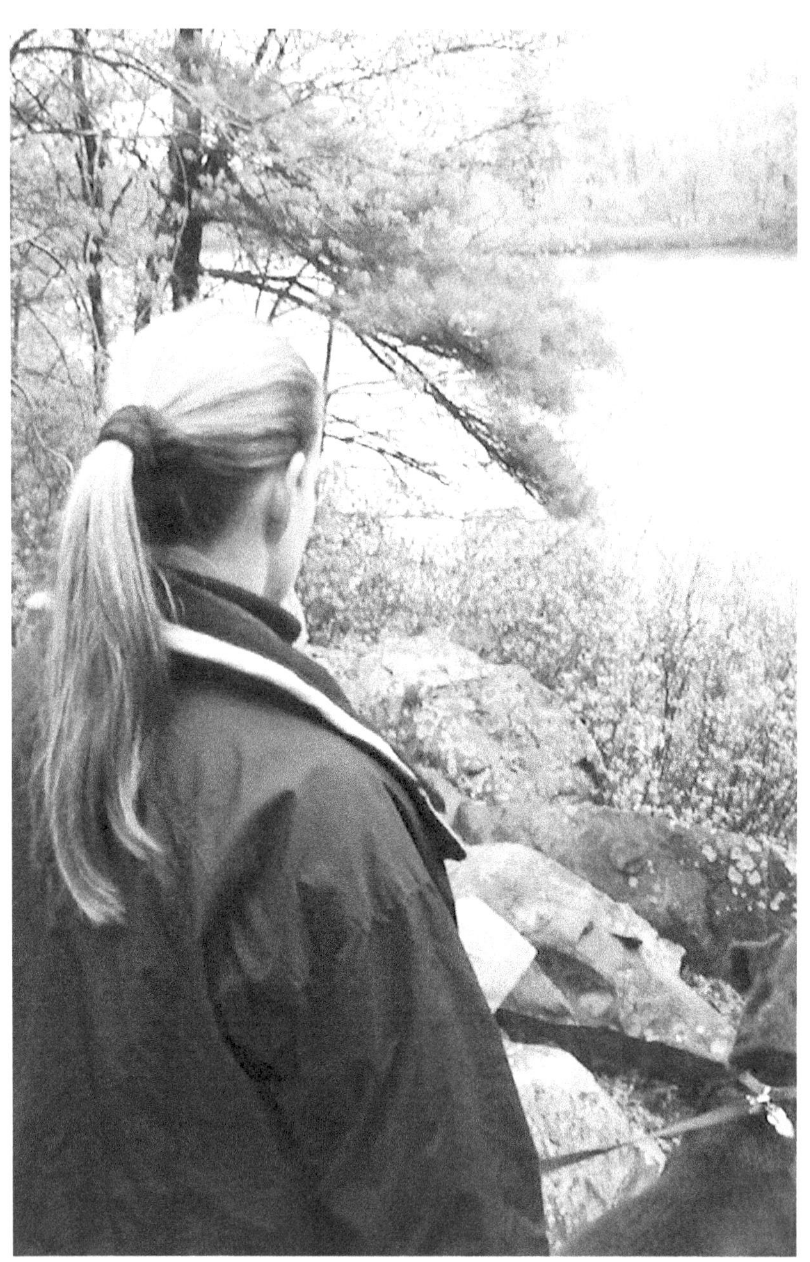

Hoops and Hurdles

Hoops and Hurdles

Who are we
as we emerge kicking
and screaming from the womb?
Parents, siblings, family, friends, enemies,
environment, economics, twisted fate, and cosmic
churnings notwithstanding are we who "we" are from the
moment of conception?

Sperm assaults egg
and person number eight billion,
five million, seven hundred fifty-nine
thousand begins. We float in a perfect universe
—serenity, security, warmth, and nourishment. Instant
gratification without having to lend voice to a single need.
Then, on some capricious signal, we're forced on a
treacherous journey through the birth canal. In
danger of choking on our own lifeline.
Cruelly ejected. Evicted. Is there
a harsher reality? Is this not
sufficient angst for
one lifetime?

Allowing for the
occasional bumps and jostles
of our fellow travelers on this earthly
planet isn't the best game plan just to get on with it?
If we lose the guilt, the second guessing, self-analysis,
self-improvement, self-imposed hoops and hurdles,
should we, can we, accept the "we" we are
on arrival? Ultimately, do we
have a choice?

There doesn't appear to be a way back in.

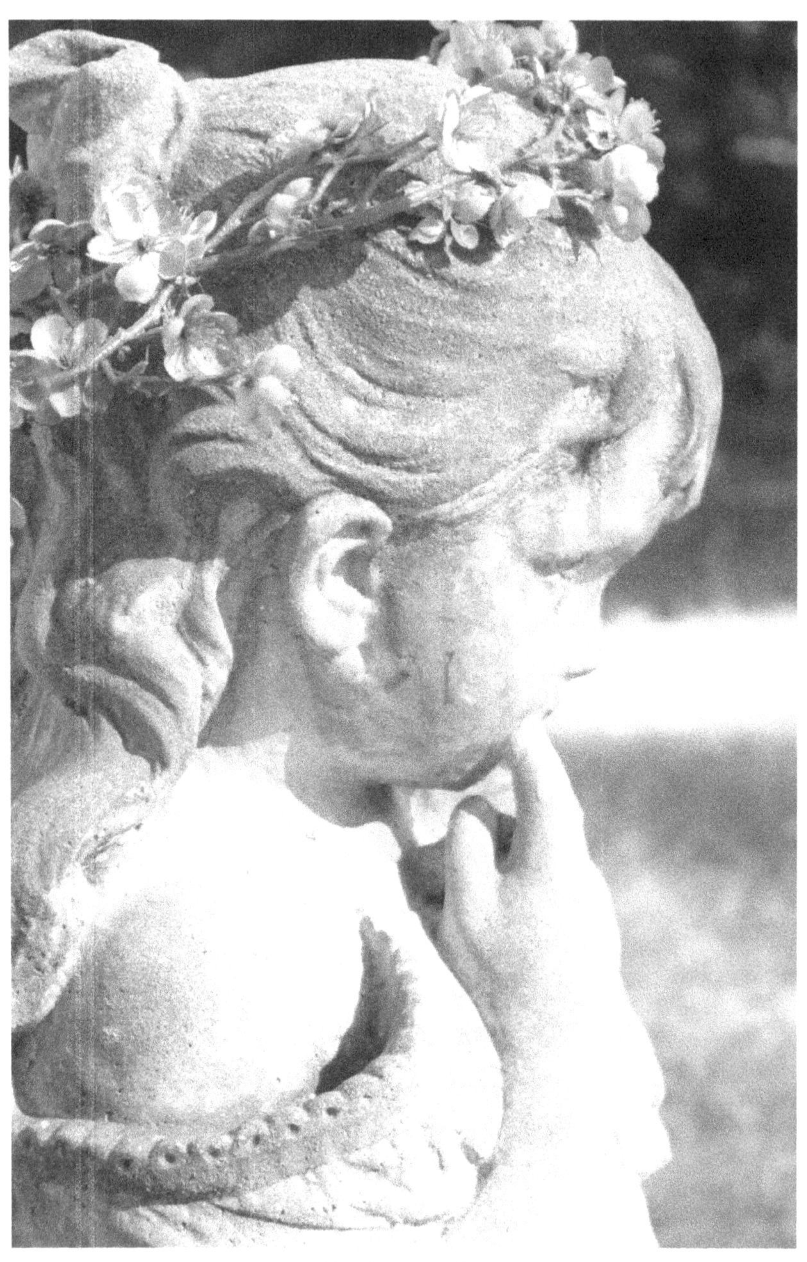

Who's On First

Who's On First

I had a name. I'm sure I did. It's here somewhere in
the back closet of my mind, third shelf from the
left, or was it the right? Behind the stack
of guest towels neatly folded, ready
for the next visitor be they
king or queen.

My name? This form calls for: last name
first, first name in the middle,
and middle initial
last.

I had a middle name once, but it must have been
revoked on my marriage certificate and
replaced with my maiden name,
following my spouse's
last name,
first.

With gold band upon third finger, left hand, my first name
vanishes betwixt and between. My new surname
debuts as my first. To wit:
Congratulations,
Mrs. Smith.

Adding one more devious twist to the name game, my first
name is further supplanted, prefixed with more of
my new mate's. I am the beneficiary of
matrimonial anonymity: I am
Mrs. John Smith.

Better yet ... ladies and gentlemen, may
I present ... Mrs. John David Smith!

Ah, a middle name; alas,
it is not mine.

With one grand flourish of the ministerial wand my
persona is transformed. I have a new set of
nomenclature. I am reincarnated.
Rediscovered. Reborn.

Simplicity itself, this evolving issue of
First/Middle/Maiden/Surname and
the proper order thereof. Maiden
was me before and surname
is what comes after.

The All-Supplanting Exception to the Rule: We of the
nesting wombs, who bear forth blessed bundles
of joy, are reprogrammed to respond to the
innocuous, insidious, one-name-fits-all
generic destroyer of any delusion of
individuality. From now until
the end of time, we are
Mom-MEEEE!

To distinguish me from others wading in the sea of
tiny hands, feet, and open mouths, I forgo my
matrimonial affiliation for my child's:
Hello. I am Danielle's mother.
Yes, I'm Becca's mom.
I'm with Heather.

Why then, with such a grand assortment of honorific
titles, do I still have twinges, yearnings for the
illusive me and seek someone, anyone
to address me by my real, if
somewhat archaic, birth
name? First, middle
and last if you
please.

Proposal: From this day forward, now and forever more, all
persons of any gender shall retain their given first,
middle, and last names, in birth order. Said
names are to be irrevocable, irreversible
and shall not be abridged, or annexed
by virtue of marriage, divorce,
death, or delivery.

Meanwhile, I remain in pursuit of the name to put in the
space marked: First Name last. I hang in there
optimistic in the belief that one day a light
will dawn. I will take pen in hand,
fill in the blank, and rejoice
that I have finally
arrived back on
First.

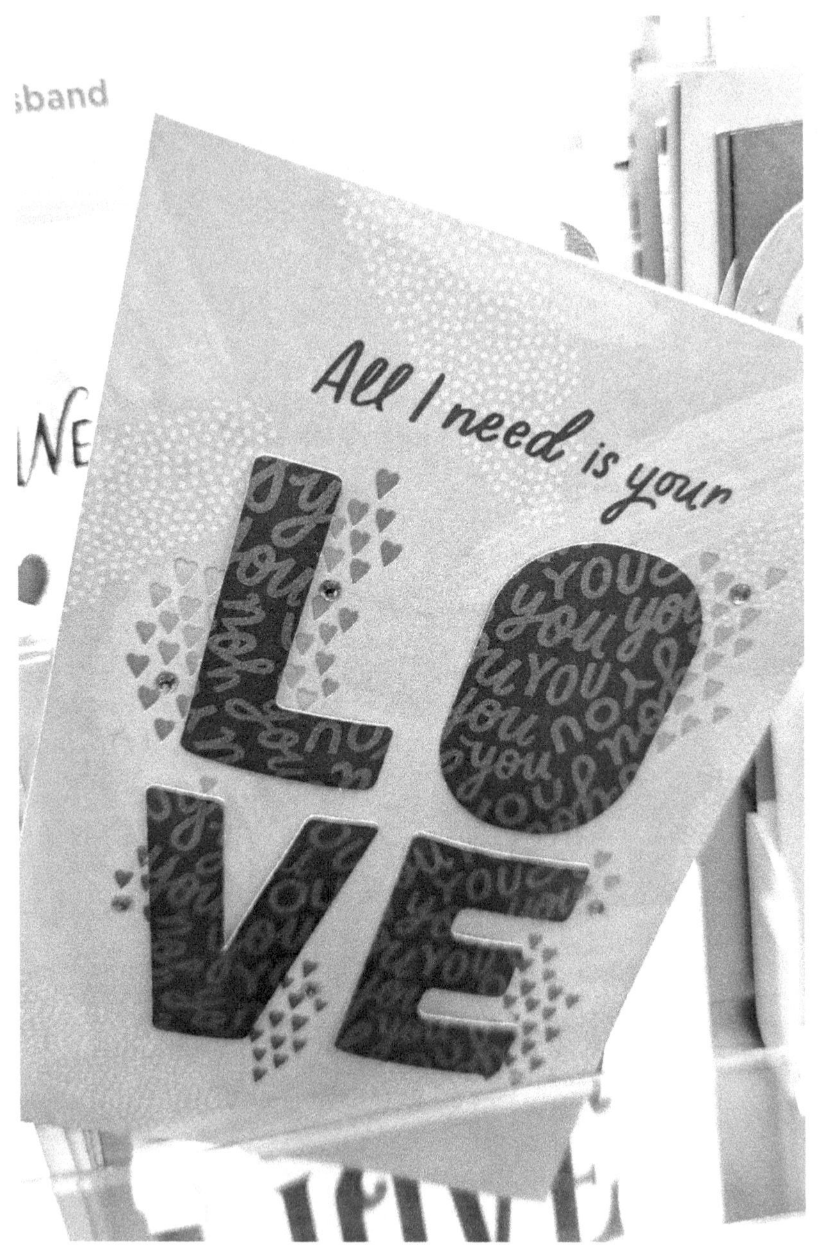

Giggles and Groans

Giggles and Groans

Lordy, lordy, I of forty am leading you astray.
Who am I to shake this paragon of perfection
and control who impresses me so?

Not for us the pangs of missed phone calls,
close encounters in movies, passionate kisses
in public. No? Not for us?

But lordy, lordy, I *am* forty and need to shout
and run and laugh and revel in love's glories.

Not for the young this awe of love for they know
not how to savor love's exquisite subtleties. To
stroke hands over a lifetime of textures—the
delicate whisper of a lover's touch, sending
quivers to the core of your being.

Oh, yes, my love, falling in love at forty is
giggles and groans. And aren't we unbelievably
lucky to have stumbled through love's
secret door?

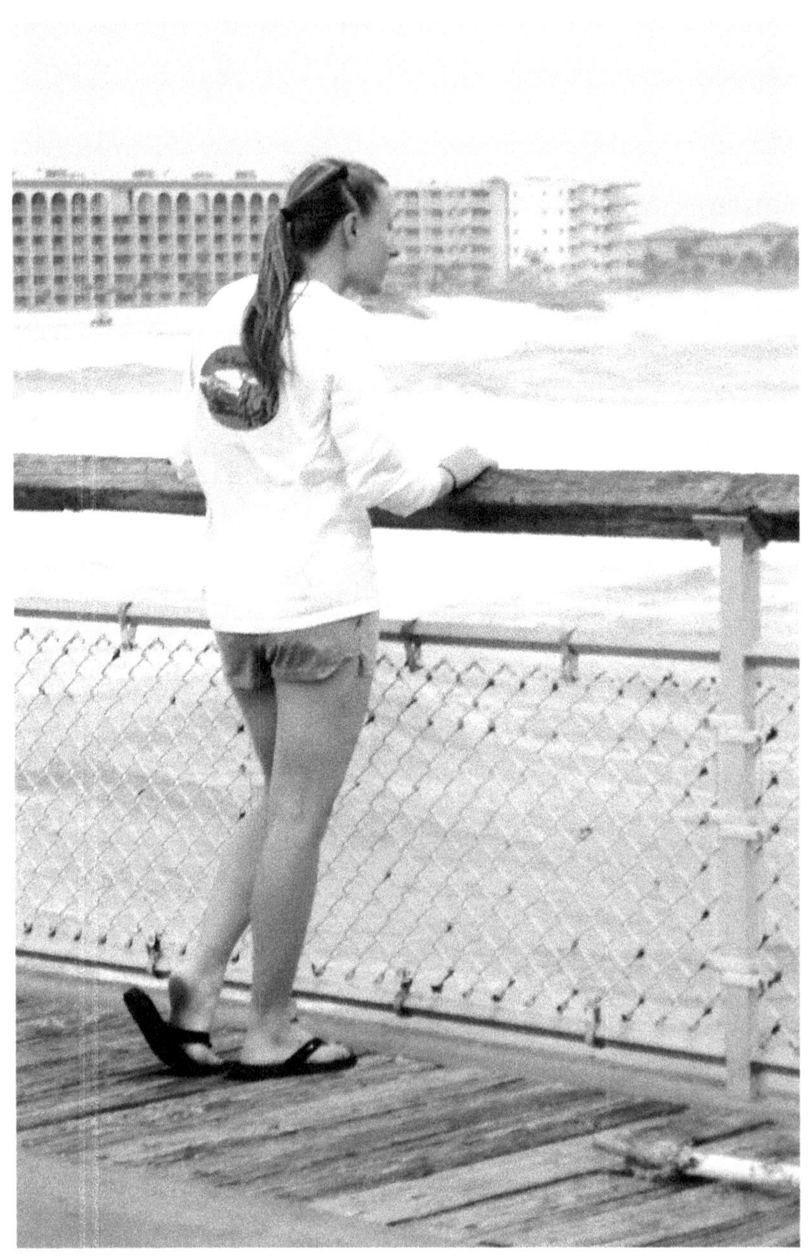

Trust

Trust

Forgive my prodding, my
poking at your heart. I did
not mean to plough through.
Rather, I sought to help you
listen to its stirrings.

My love for you this day is
confident and sure. I am
impatient to go on. *Slow
down*, proceed with *caution*
—difficult for me with you.

I will linger longer here for
this love—yours and mine, but
I need your hand to hold, your
heart to know to move with
you from this day to the next.

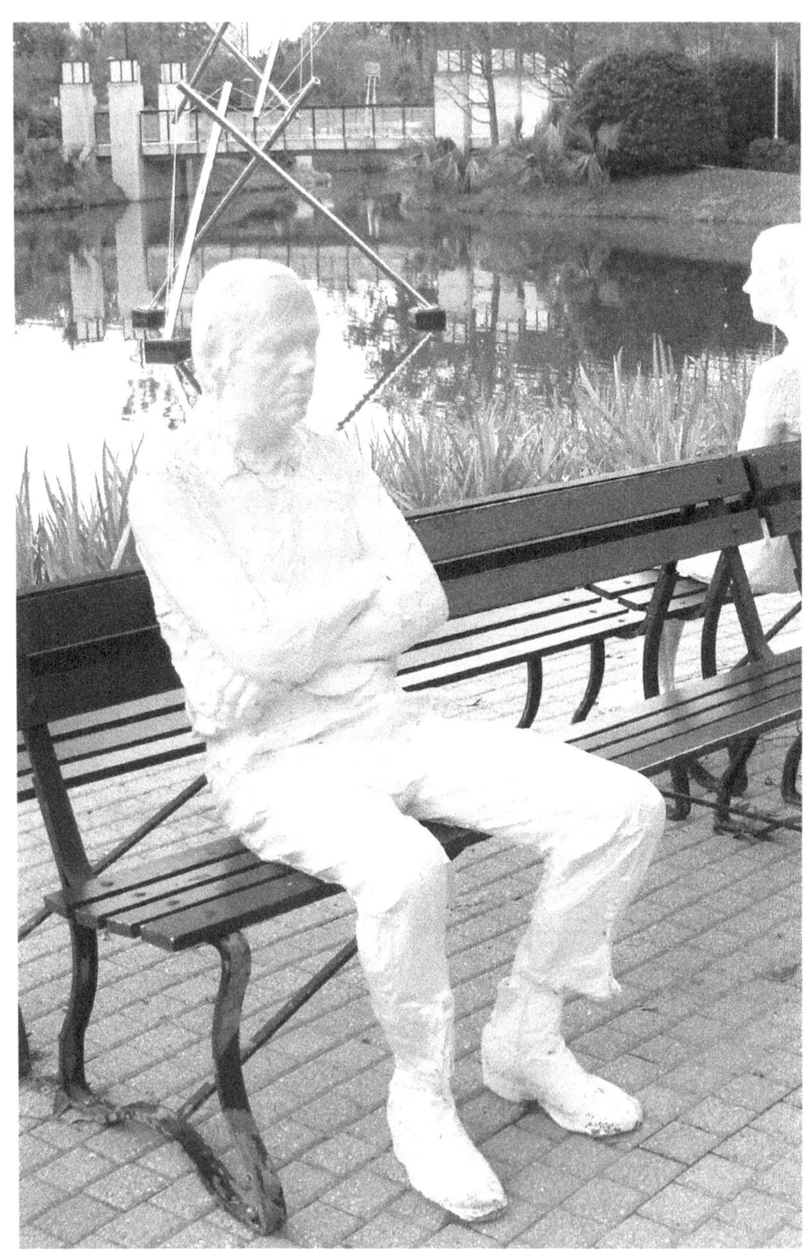

Close Apart

Close Apart

(A Sad Dolly Parton Country Song)

We're in this together so close apart.
We make love with passion,
but not with our hearts.

We fell in as partners like Bonnie and Clyde,
but no death-do-us-part pledge
binds us side-by-side.

If I left tomorrow no tear would be shed,
for first you must notice,
I'm not in our bed.

We're in this together so close apart.
We make love with passion,
but not with our hearts.

So, what's this we have here my housemate,
my friend? A non-working arrangement
it's time to amend.

A trip down the aisle or hold status quo.
A toss up, a guess dear,
keep me: *Yes/No?*

We're in this together so close apart.
We make love with passion
but not with our hearts.

I'm greedy, not desperate, begging
I'll forego, If you've had enough,
Then speak and say so.

Too much effort? How sad.
True love, once looming,
now, not to be had.

We were in this together so close apart.
We made love with passion,
And now we do part

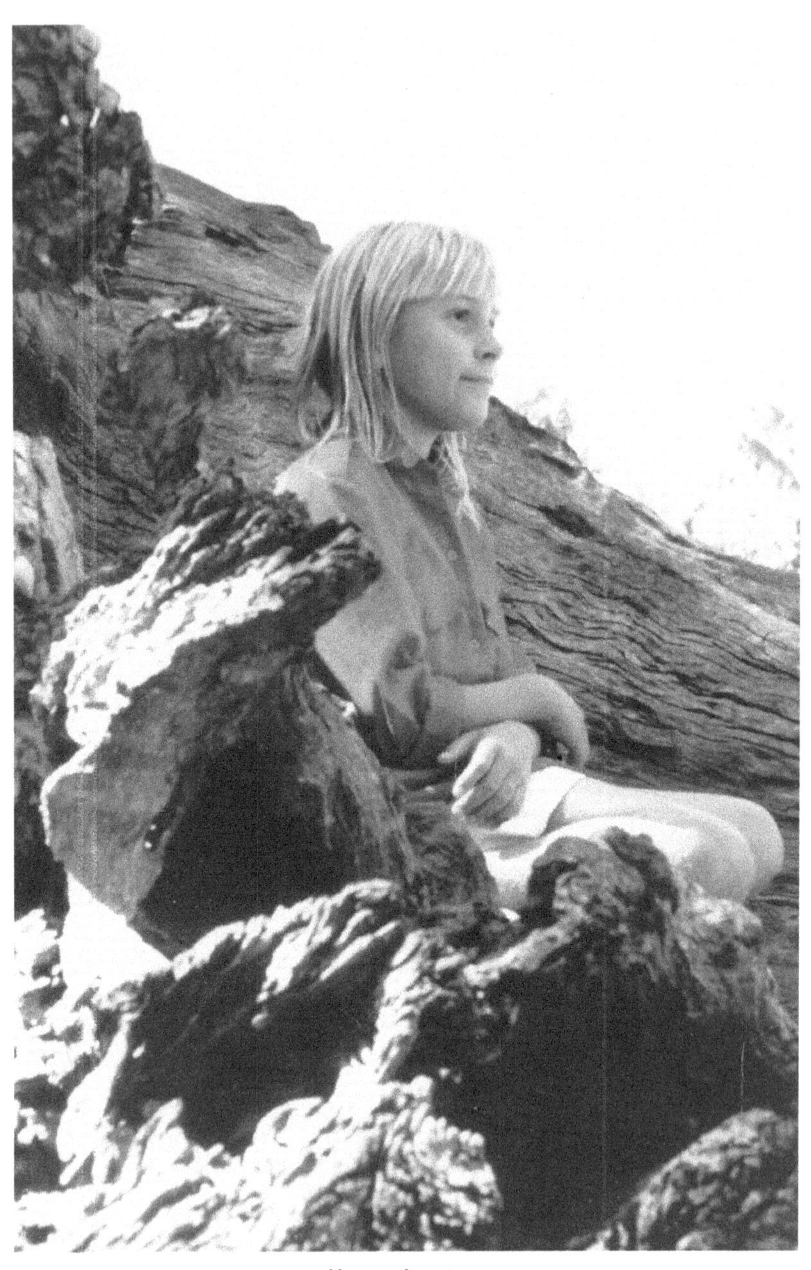

File Baby Lost
Photo by artist Glinda Schafer

File: Baby Lost

A stranger moved in. Size/Shape: Under Construction.
I should know her, but we really haven't met.
Her schedule is at odds with mine.

Daily Agenda:
    One *No show*
      Two *Confrontations*
        Three *I'll-see-you-laters*
          Four *You-don't-understands.*

My twelve-year-old poltergeist hurtles towels, scatters
food-encrusted dishes over, under, and on every available
surface, simultaneously commandeering remote controls,
video games, and tablets.

Her cohorts answer to *Pug, Mouse,* and *Little Bit.* Appearing
unannounced, they just as magically disappear into the black
hole of my little one's former fairy-tale bedroom.

My baby has vanished. A stranger lurks within.
Occasionally, a shadow of someone
I once knew whiffs by ....

Blessed is she who remains unaware of the pitfalls of her
quest for she carries not the mantle of fear. My precious little
one may you safely soar through turbulent skies
on your journey from tween to teen.

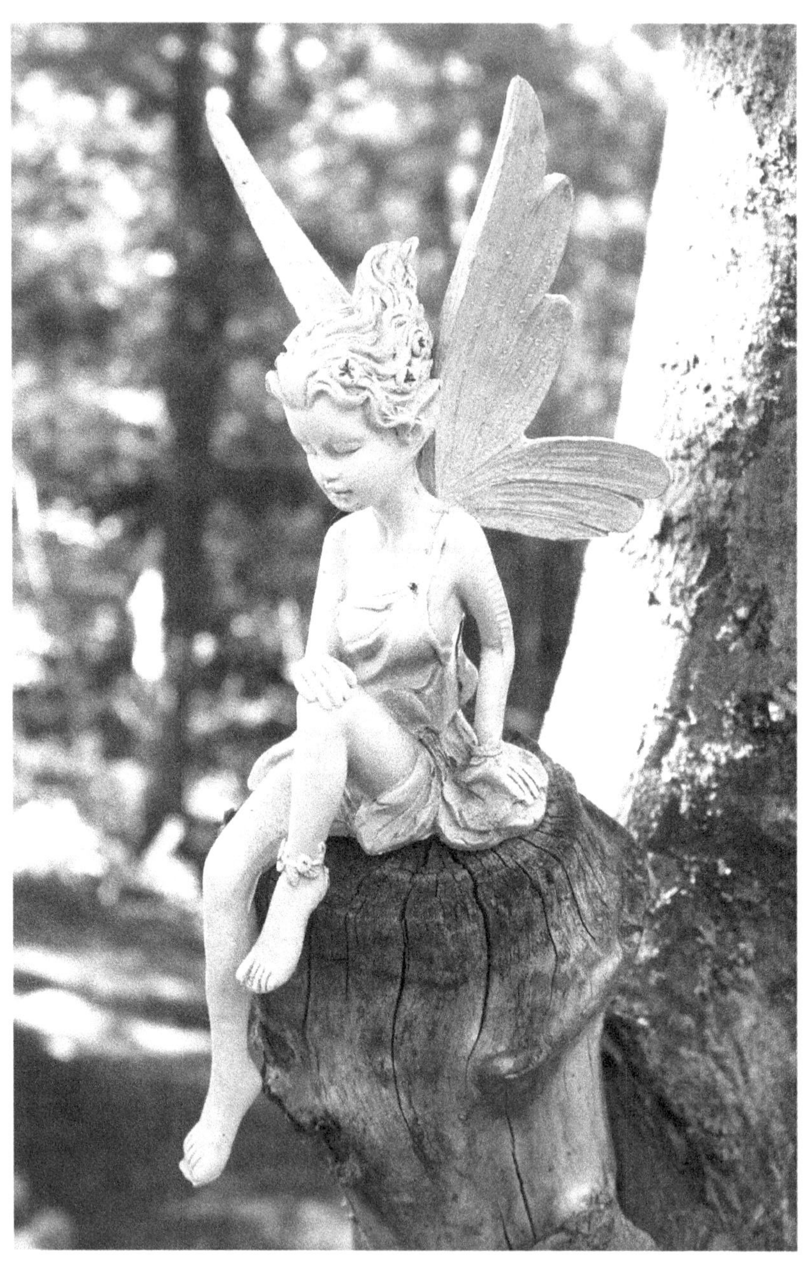

Fairy Wood Nymph

Fairy Wood Nymph

Darting among the wildflowers, a whisper
slipping from tree to tree, gliding across
the green, green moss. Friend and protector
to all who call the forest home.

Diving into the Pool of Cool Water, bubbling
up to dance beneath its cascading waterfall,
your boundless curiosity unfolds. Quietly you
stole my heart with an impish smile.

Danielle Dawn, I knew you before you were
born. Emerging from my dream, bringing the
enchantment of your fairy kingdom to share
with a mere mortal.

My lovely Fairy Wood Nymph, you have birthed
your own, and in your role as mother and
nurturer, you have excelled, bestowing
wisdom, kindness, and joy!

—To Danielle Dawn with love beyond measure
from your adoring mother
                    Mother's Day 05/12/2024

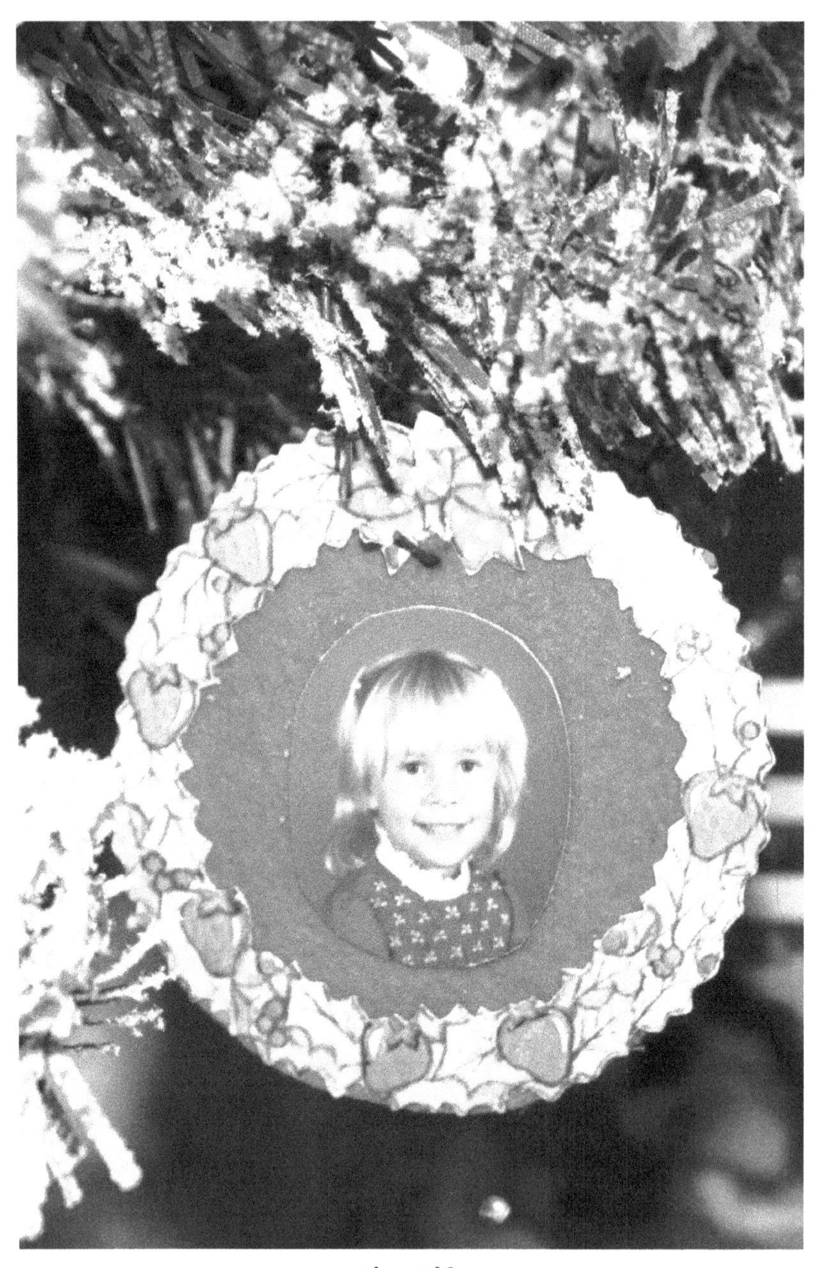

The Gift

The Gift

I lie here underneath the Christmas
tree to remind my family
I am the Gift.

I'm the youngest, the baby, so
to speak. My will, will
not be thwarted.

No curling ribbons or fancy paper
necessary. My cherubic self is
sufficiently sufficient.

You will indulge me. You will
smile. For after all,
I am the Gift.

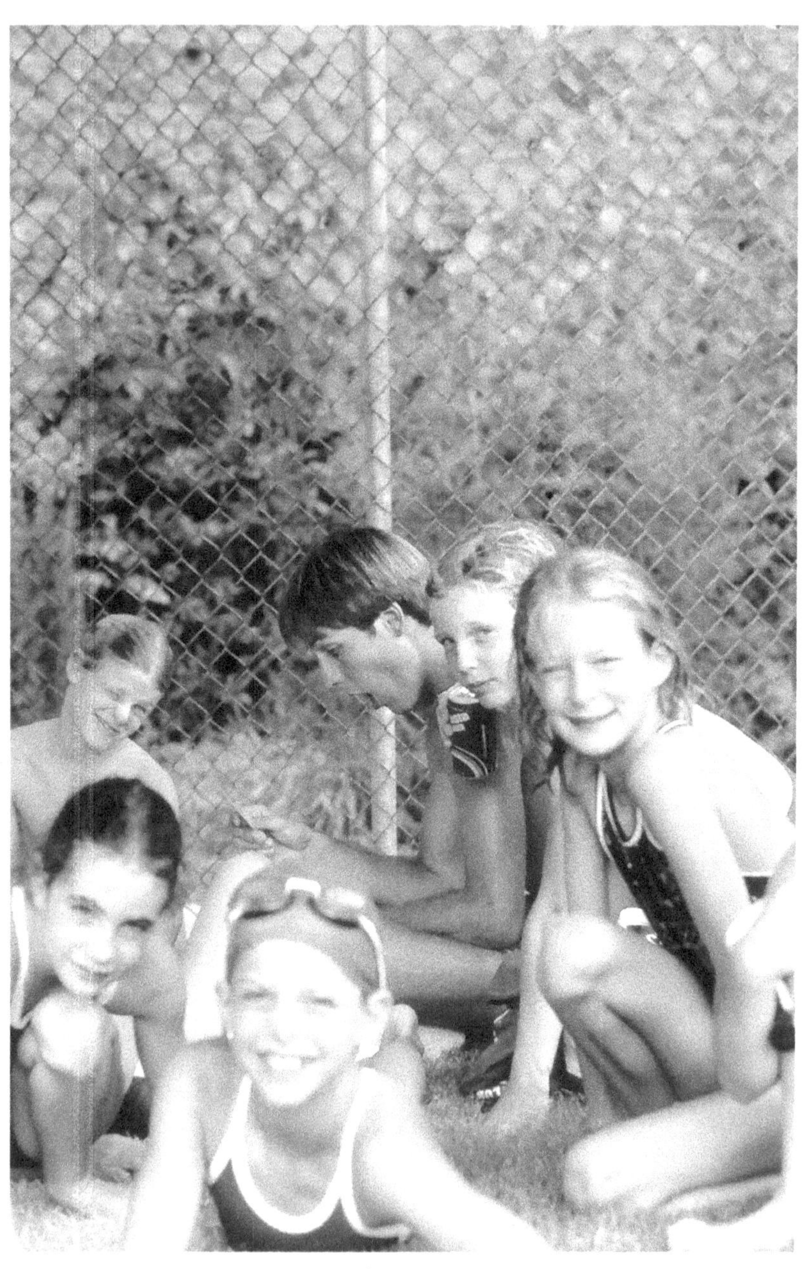

Swim Mate

Swim Mate

You know you've bumped into a swim mate when ... their wrinkled, peeling skin bumps into yours, and you are not repulsed. The distinct fragrance of *Eau de Chlorine* wafts by.

Together you sport identical hairstyles down to the last bleached out, dried out, frizzed out strand, tinted a matching shade of "Pool Green."

Without question, you acknowledge that the gouge marks around your new friend's eyes are from goggles, not some weird fetish to imitate Ronnie the Raccoon.

Blindfold you can recite the contents of the swim bag he/she drags around:
   4 caps—all sporting different logos
   3 faded, shot-with-holes practice suits
   2 pairs of don't-you-dare-touch or adjust my goggles
   1 crumbling chocolate chip cookie
   1 empty shampoo bottle, wrapped inside a slightly damp
      smelly towel and
   1 illegible "love-note" from your coach.

On comparing practice sets, you take a form of masochistic pride in affirming your coach is a bigger ogre than his/hers. Discussing those same practice sessions, you agree that neither rain, snow, sleet, hurricane, broken bones, or death-bed rattles shall prevent aforementioned coach
from requiring your presence at practice.

Despite all the grueling, torturous, monotonous hours in and out of the water, it's all worth it. You are looking at a mirror image of the best-developed, healthiest body ever produced
by male or female because
swimmers are the real thing!

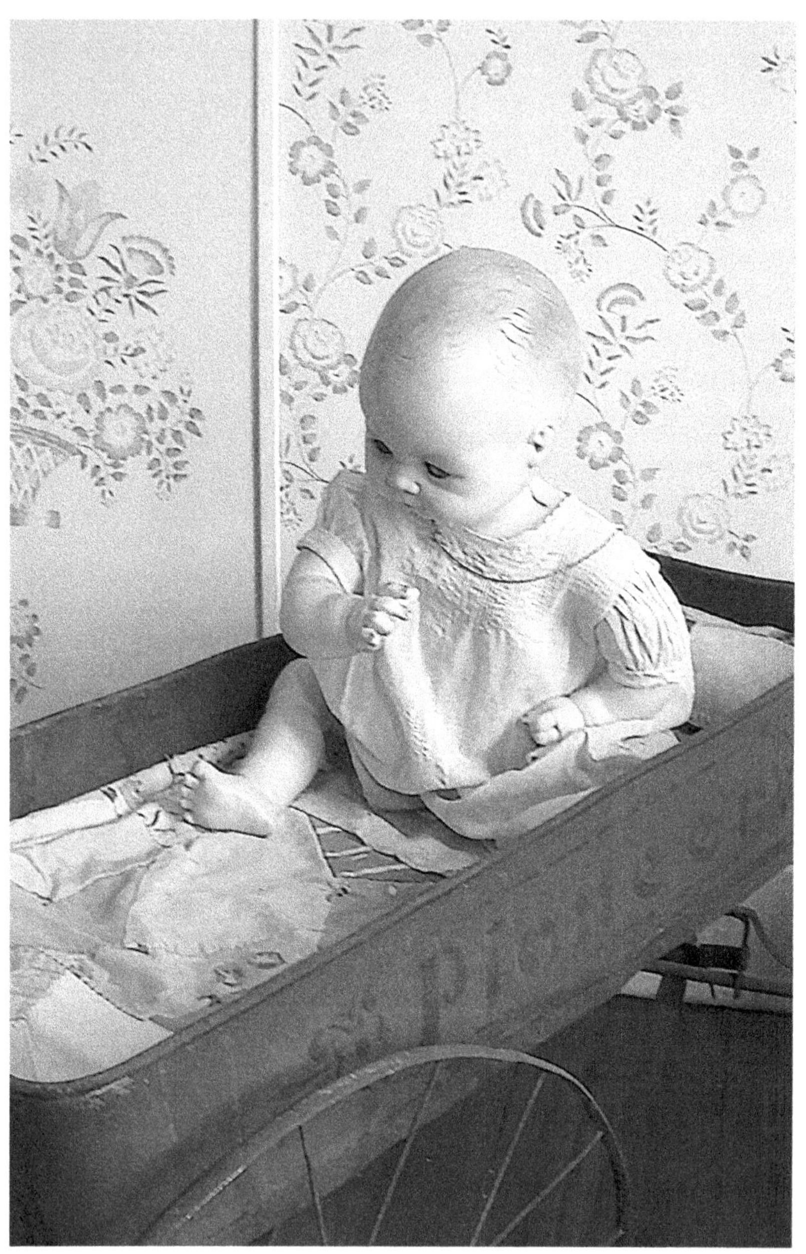

Diane

Diane

Matilda, your favorite doll—cuddled
and loved even as her rubber skin
dried and cracked.
I remember.

A music box ballerina twirling in dizzying
arabesques. Mason jars, catching fireflies
on a summer's eve. Honeysuckle branches
laden with golden flowers—secret fairy
cubbyholes hidden from world.
I remember.

The narrow stream wiggling through the
backyard. Rock dam in summer, big enough
for two small butts. Winter, four-bladed shoe
skates scooting awkwardly on a frozen path.
I remember.

Bobbsey Twins and *Nancy Drew*, solving crimes
along with them. The closet-door mirror, an
improvised camera for special sister Sunday-
after-mass television shows. Clever art lessons
(you) and commercial breaks (me).
I remember.

Lake George, bats in the kitchen, cats in the
rafters, raccoons on the patio, diving for trash
can covers in clear lake waters. Dad at the helm
of a rented speed boat.
I remember.

Matching uniforms: grammar school navy blue
jumpers, powder blue Peter Pan-collared blouses.
High school Kelly green, box pleats and penny
loafers. Hour bus rides across the Hudson and back.
I remember.

The Everly Brothers, Elvis, Jan and Dean on 45s,
record player stored in the built-in bookcase of
our shared partner's desk.
I remember.

White princess prom dress, blue sashed waist,
posing proudly on the arm of Pat, boyfriend and
future husband. *Moon River* forever enshrined.
I remember.

Diane Carol, sister and best friend, evermore the
keeper of my most cherished childhood memories.
I remember you.

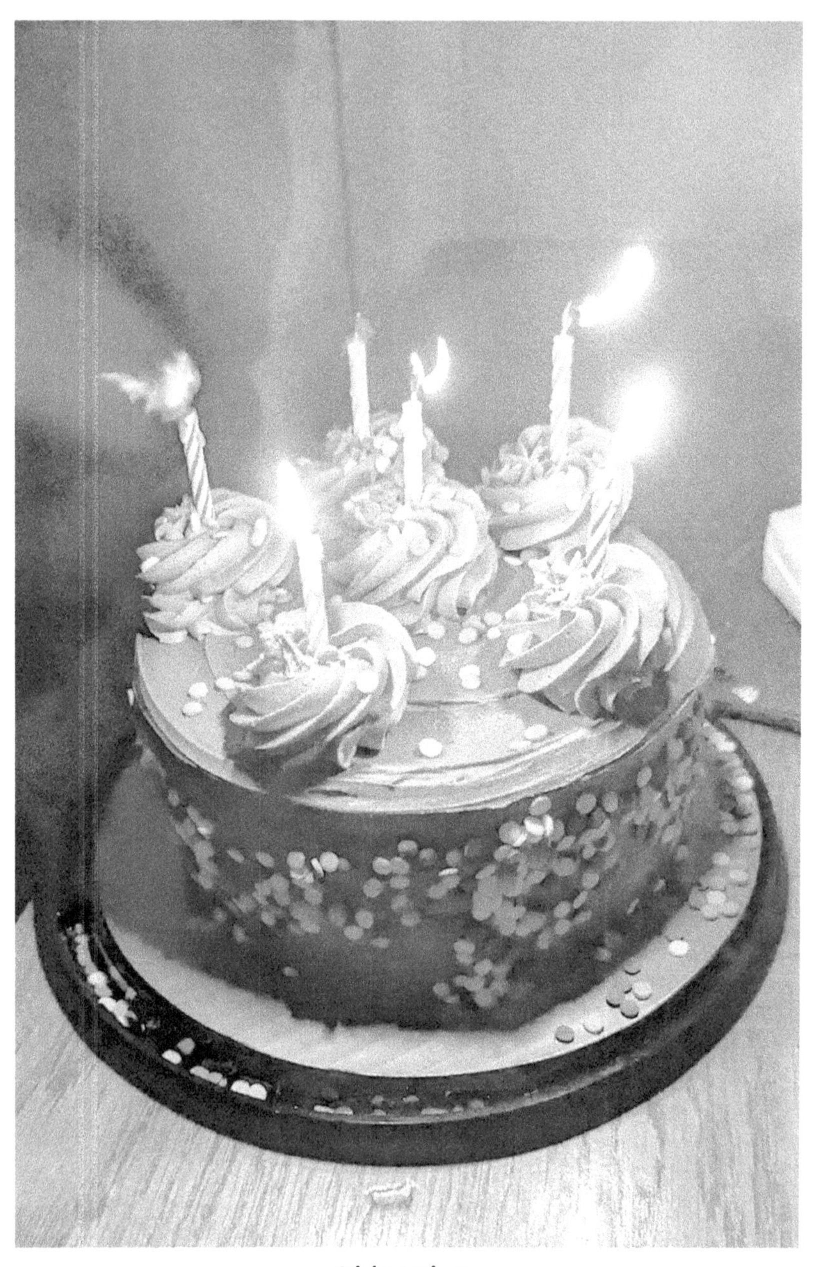

Older Than

Older Than

You there, I here. Older
than my father? How
did I pass him by?

What misaligned universe
slipped one billionth of a
millimeter off axis and
rendered your offspring
decades older than you?

How does a daughter
crinkle with wrinkles,
while the parent who
begot the child never
knows such afflictions?

April Fools Day—the birthday
where you don't age. How
disquieting to celebrate
you at forty-two.

The photo of a robust strikingly
handsome man stares back. The
father of my youth reaches out
through time and comforts me.

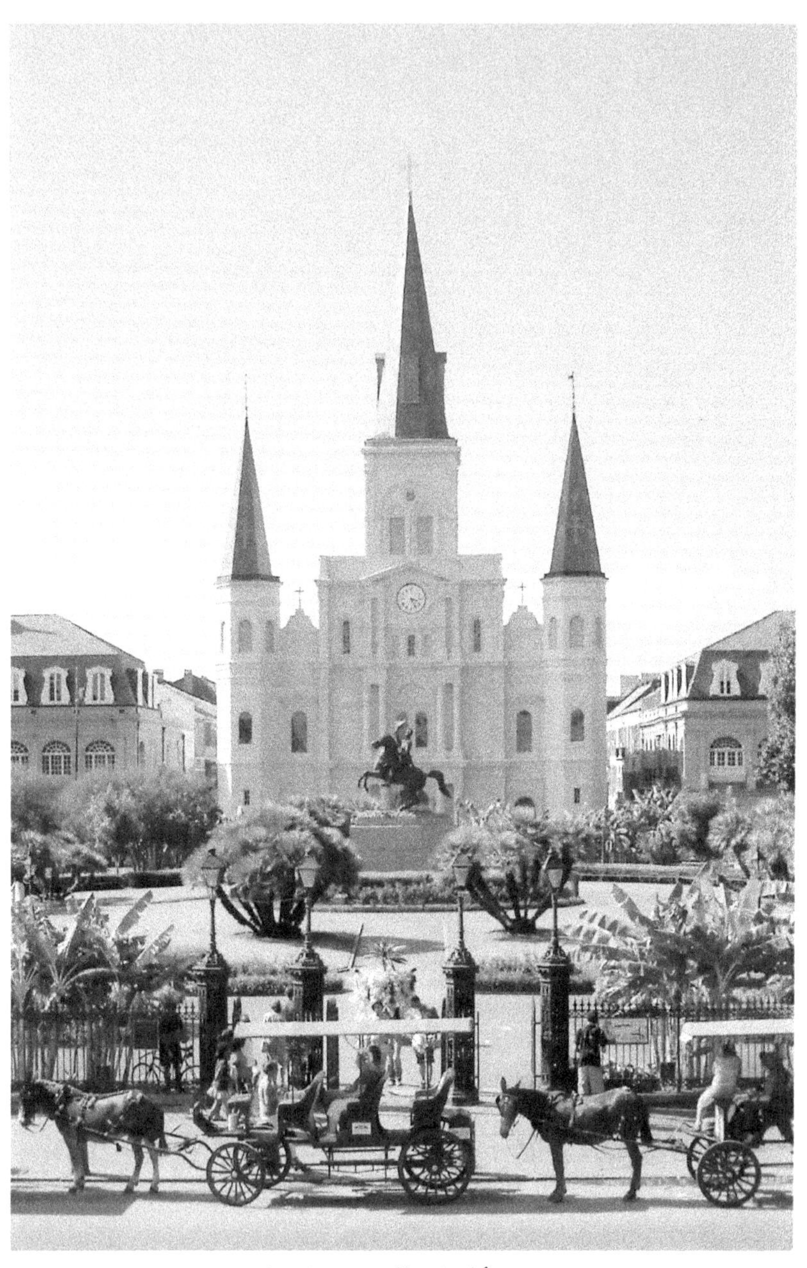

La Nouvelle Orléans

La Nouvelle Orléans

Wandering through the old Quarter, *le Vieux Carré,* the
music fills your soul. *Laissez les bon temps roulez—*
let the good times roll.

Spicy aromas mingle, permeating the air: beignets,
café au laît, king cake, jambalaya spicy and hot,
crawfish and gumbo bubbling in the pot.

Sizzling sunshine tenders warming rays. Brick-lined
courtyards lush with shade—cooling hideaways
on those blazing summer days.

Along the Moonwalk, the mighty Mississippi churns on by.
Tugboats, tankers, steamboats navigate the whirling
twists and turns under your watchful eye.

Down hidden bayous, pirogues glide on dew drops, pelicans
swoop, egrets preen, lurking alligators slip beneath
murky waters awaiting their prey.

At *le fais do do, the* raucous notes of *Iko Iko* swirl through
starry skies. Beaucoup friends and family join in all the fun.
The winning hand in *Bourré* laughs at his lucky run.

"Second lines," invitations to dance in the streets.
In *Nouvelle Orléans,* the "City that care forgot,"
joy is the only creature you meet.

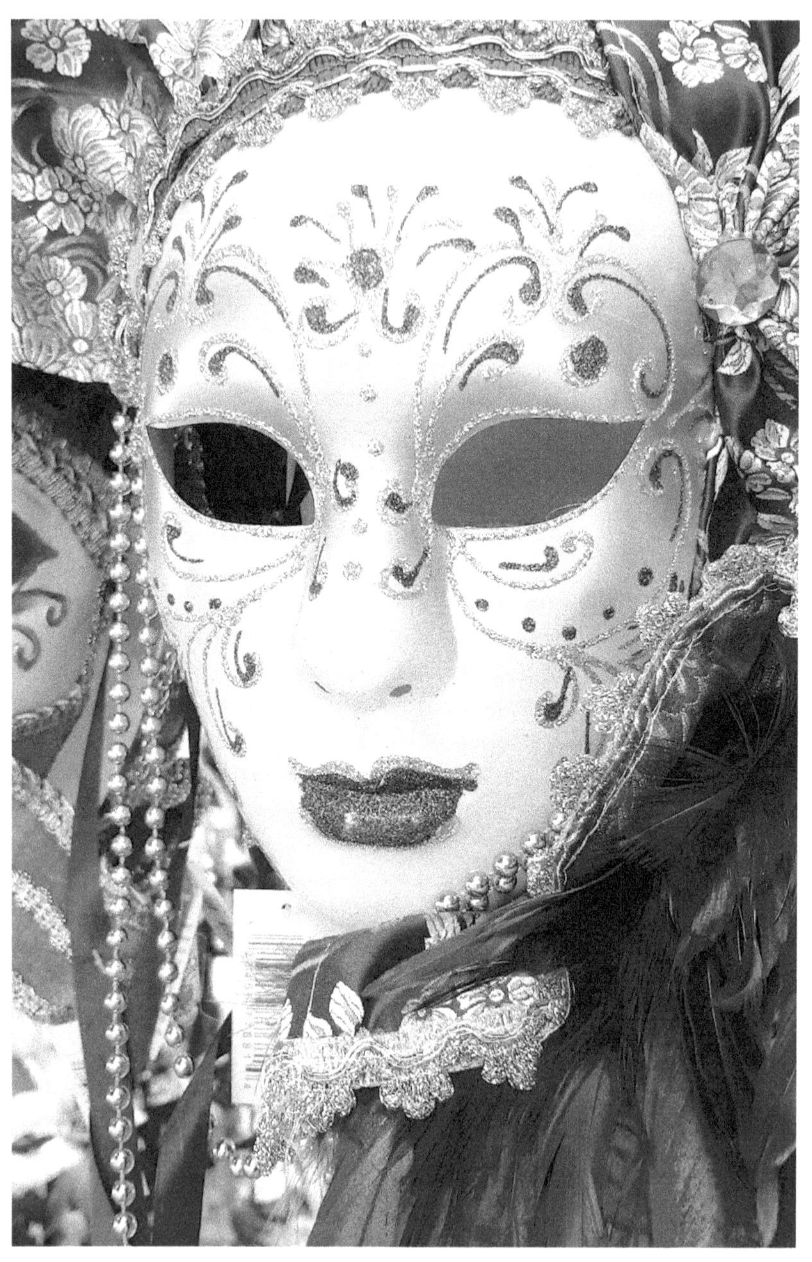

Carnival Time

Carnival Time

Boobs, bangles,
      beads, and butts.
Carnival jangles,
      careens and struts.

A second line through
      stale beer streets,
a bevy of maskers
      doles out treats.

Balconies, bars,
      curbside squats,
the view spews forth
       dysfunctional shots.

Clang of cymbals,
      thud of drums,
blare of horns,
      cracked musical crumbs.

Incoherent,
      disjointed discord,
it's Carnival time,
      all revelers on board!

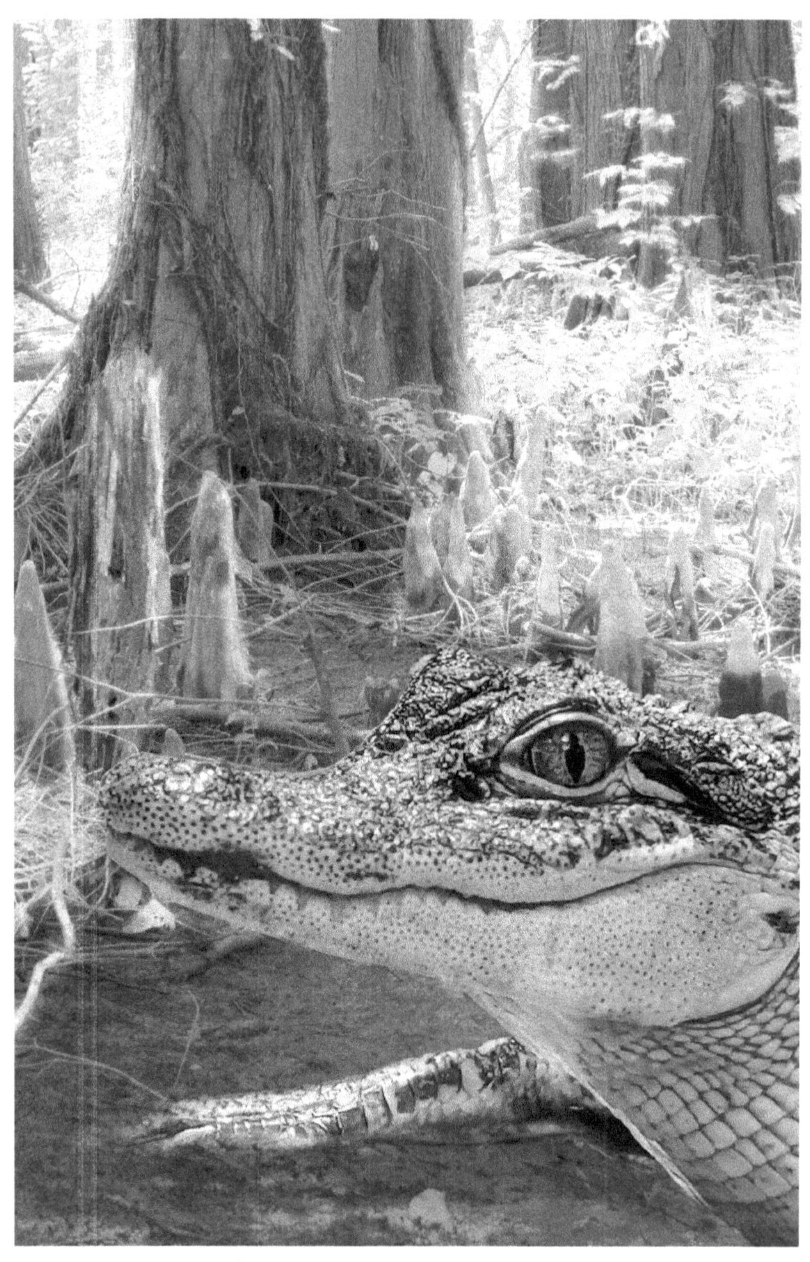

Random Thoughts from the Bayou
Photo by Patrick Eul

Random Thoughts from the Bayou

The goal of all true professionals is
to thoroughly analyze all situations,
anticipate potential problems, and
move swiftly to resolve same—prior
to occurrence.

However ...

When you are up to your ass in
alligators, it's difficult to remember
that your initial objective was to drain
the swamp.

Options: Slay the Gator.
         Fry the Gator
         Eat the Gator

Recipe: 2 pounds gator tail cut into chunks. Dredge
chunks in buttermilk. In large bowl, double dredge
gator chunks in flour, seasoned with salt, cayenne
pepper, heavy on the garlic powder. In large cast iron
skillet, fry gator in oil till golden brown, approximately
4 to 5 minutes.
Dipping sauce: mix equal amounts Tabasco sauce,
horseradish, ketchup, and lemon juice. Serve hot.
Wash down with cold beer, preferably Abita. Alas, Jax
and Dixie are no longer made.

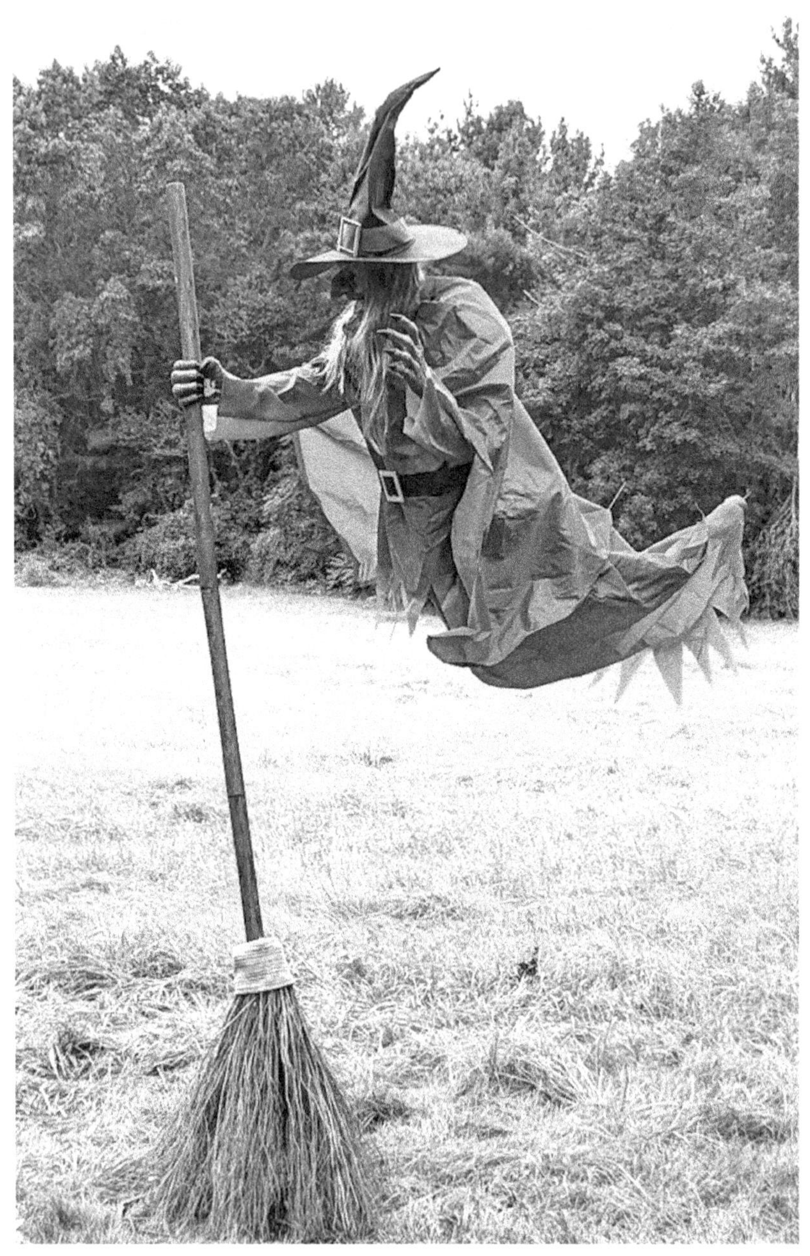

Witches Brew

Witches Brew

If I were a witch and
you were a warlock
would there be room
for you on my broom?

No, I think not,
for your presence
would impede
my quintessential
need for speed.

Warlocks and others of
like ilk should be found
feet planted firmly
on the ground.

The sisterhood rejects
the tether to earth-bound
men. We prefer to commune
sailing past the harvest moon.

Potions and spells bring
forth the evil eye.
Better you wave
as I fly by.

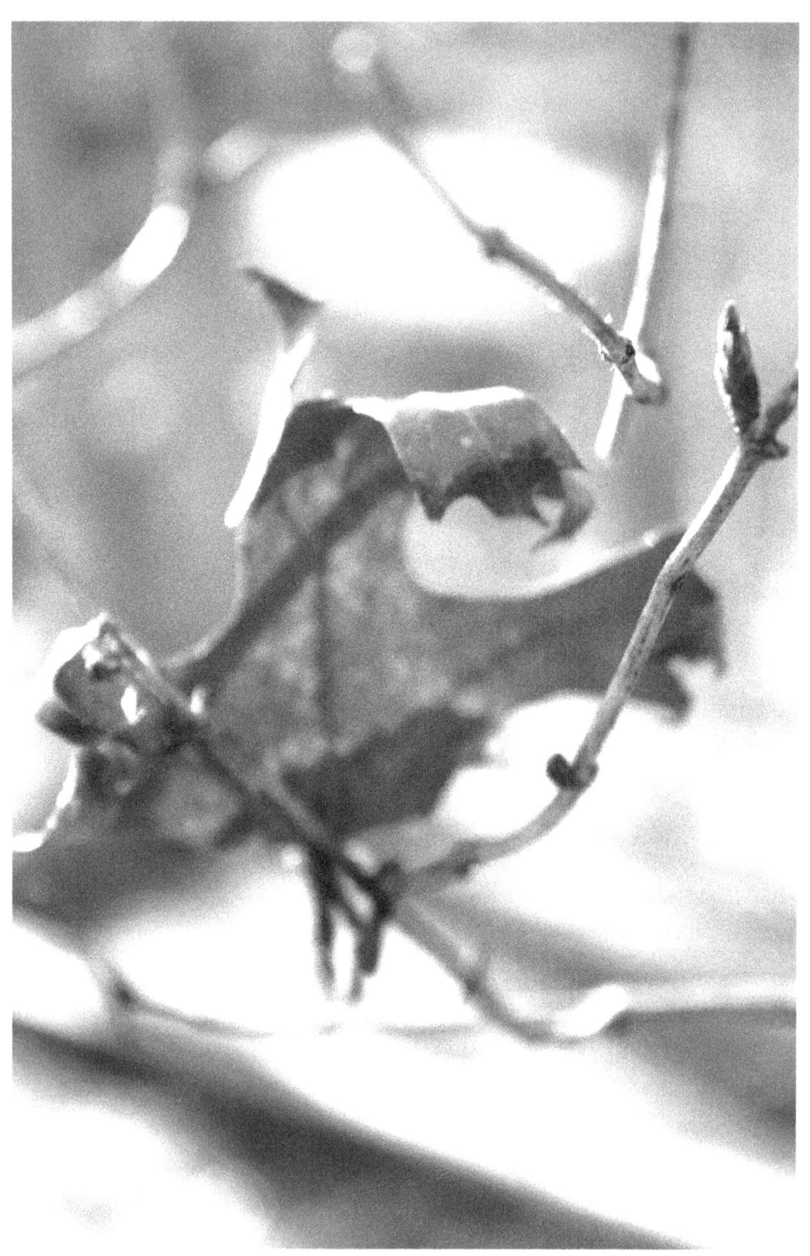

Magic

Magic

A leaf sailed by today, a flawlessly folded

origami bird. I wanted to give chase

but this enchanted being had

already skittered back to

the flock. I will never

catch my origami

bird. Magic isn't

meant to be

caged.

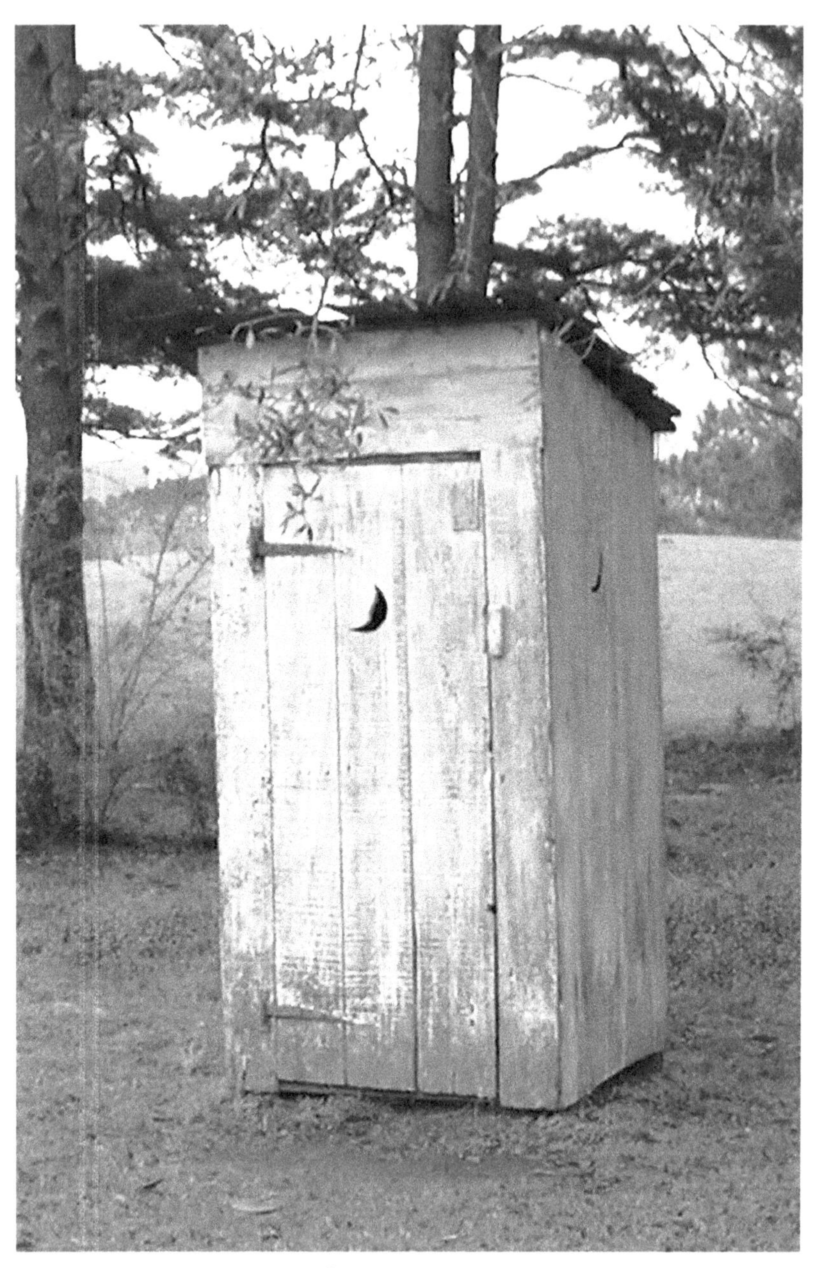

The Necessary

The Necessary

Pity the user of the solitary potty,
spiders, flies, creepy crawlies, odors
rank, cleanliness spotty.

What's behind that door—one
hole two holes, three holes, four
circle, oval, kiddy-size or more?

Star, diamond, crescent moon,
peek-a-boo cutouts call out
You'd better get here real soon.

Sun-scourged days, frozen nights
go-out-backs, pots of gold,
—always a welcome relief in sight.

Once rudimentary privies, hidey-holes
—fixtures 'or the land. Now sani-cans
and port-o-lets take on those vital roles.

Still, accolades be given where praise is due.
All hail the Necessary, hanging in there for
me and you.

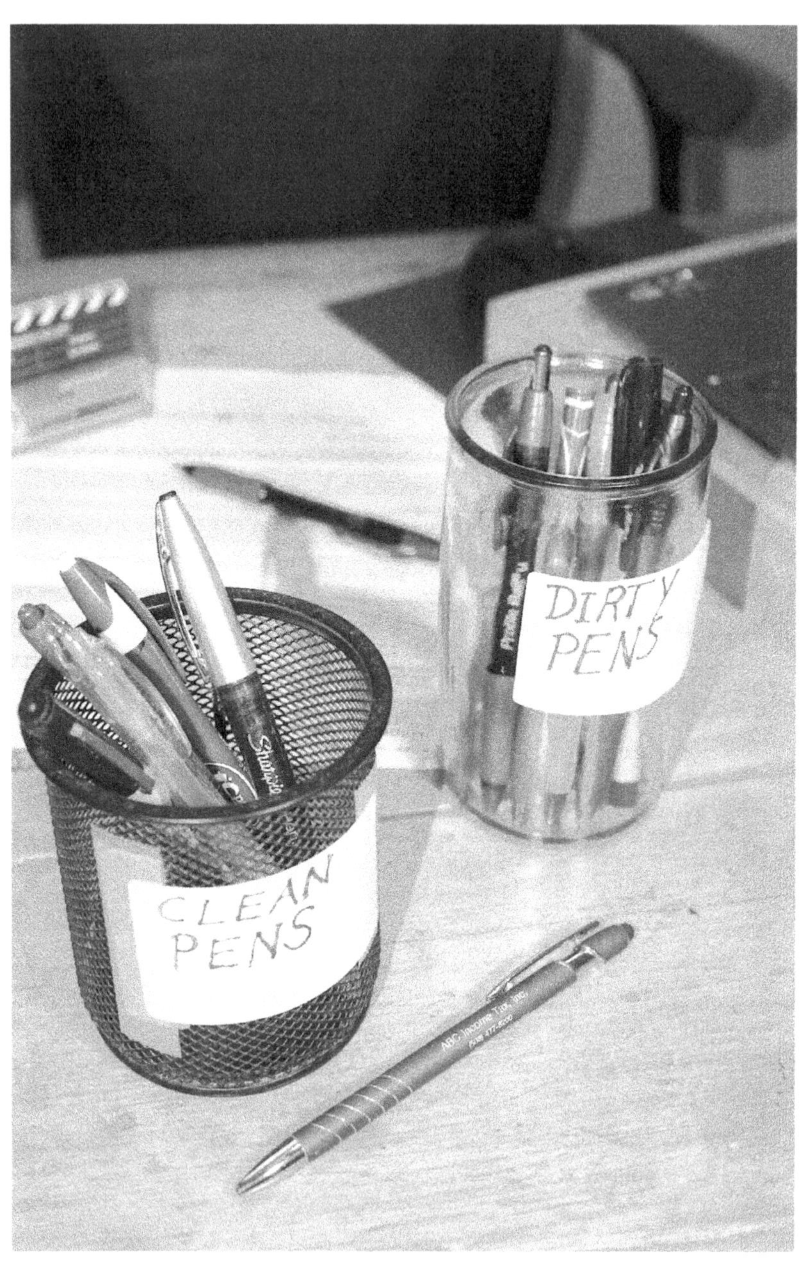

This Pen

This Pen

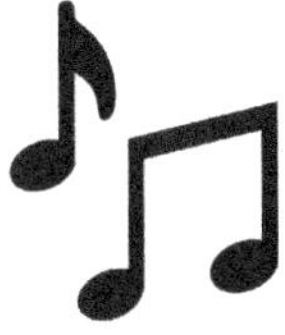

This pen is my pen. This pen is your pen.
From California to the New York island.
From the redwood forests to the
Gulf stream waters, this pen
*was made for you and me.**

STEAL: Take that which is not yours.
BORROW: Take temporary custody.

Upon signing in or filling out a form with proffered pen, and said pen subsequently falls into pocket, purse, or bag, it is understood such action does not constitute pilfering.

Nor is it to be considered a criminal offense as proffered pens are immune from prosecution. However, Covid protocol mandates that returning a Used pen into the Clean pen bin renders the offender a violator of human sensibilities.

Pens branded with company logo, address, phone number are designed to be shared. During their lifetimes these distinctive implements will travel globally across countries, continents, and yon to the nether regions of outer space. The transport agent is under no obligation to return to sender.

*To Woody Guthrie, humble apologies for commandeering your lyrics.

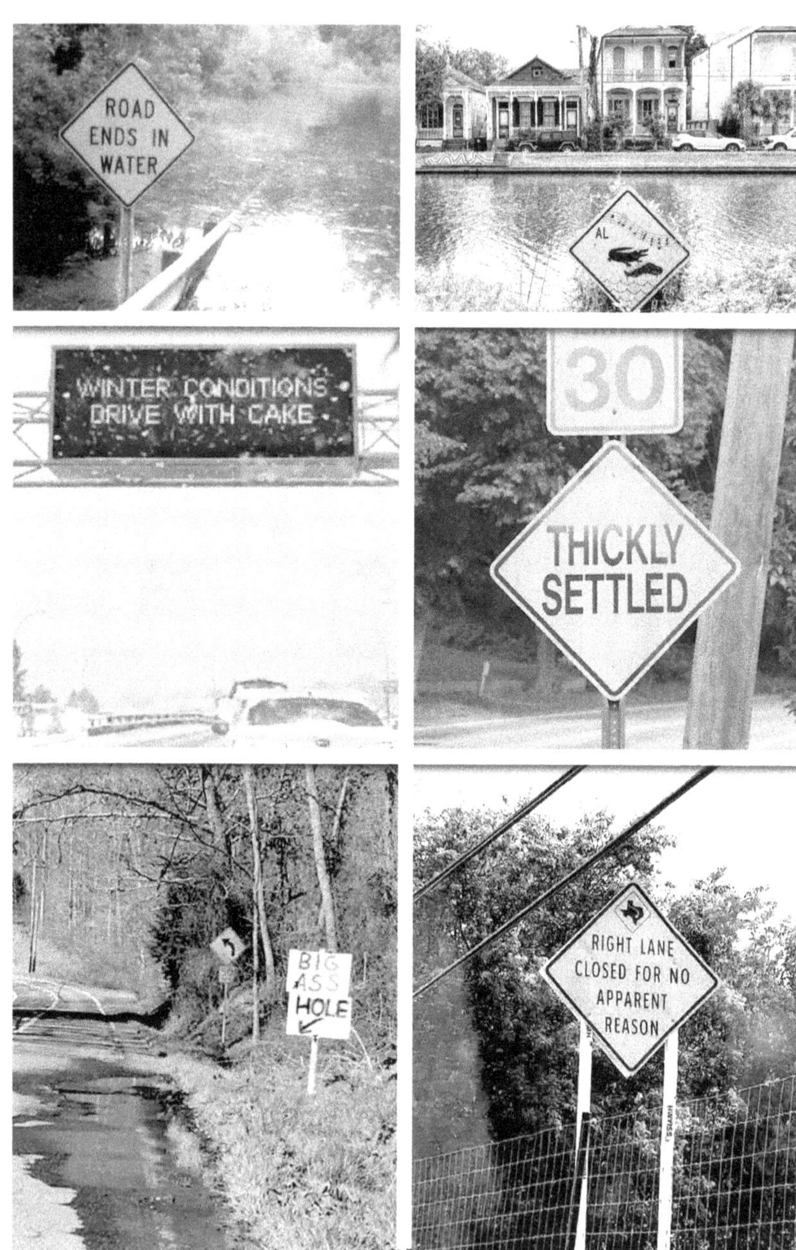

Signs to Ponder
Collage by Patrick Eul

Signs To Ponder

LOW FLYING PLANES
Duck?

FALLING ROCKS
Catch?

DENSELY POPULATED
No vacancy?

LOW SALT ZONE
Heart Healthy?

DANGEROUS INTERSECTION
Locked and Loaded?

**ACCIDENTS ARE PROHIBITED
ON THIS ROAD**
I feel so much better.

**2 HOUR PARKING
7PM TO 8PM**
You do the math.

THIS LIGHT NEVER TURNS GREEN
Ah, the parking zone for that missing second hour.

SOFT SHOULDER
Available to lean on?

ALWAYS DRIVE WITH CAKE
*A Marie Antoinette throwback as
in let them feast on sugary treats?*

**PARKING LOT UNDER POLICE
SURVEILLANCE. DO NOT LEAVE
VALUABLES IN CAR**

So not reassuring.

**NOTICE: NO SIGNS ALLOWED
            AT THIS INERSECTION**

Do as I say not as I do.

SIGN NOT IN USE

Fill in the blank?

WARNING ROAD SIGN AHEAD

The pre-warning for the warning.

**WARNING BRIDGE WASHED OUT
UNLESS YOU FEEL THIS IS AN
ATTEMPT TO DEPRIVE YOU OF
YOUR LIBERTY, THEN KEEP DRIVING**

Choices, I like it.

BEWARE WILD ANIMALS/CHILDREN

Together? On the loose?

SUICIDAL DEER NEXT ONE MILE

Number for Deer hotline?

CAUTION: ALLIGATOR CROSSING

No Problem, I know where I don't belong.

**DO STICK YOUR ELBOW OUT TOO FAR
IT MIGHT GO HOME IN ANOTHER CAR**

Poetic justice?

SLOW THE *#%*! DOWN

No translation necessary.

SOPT

Failed spelling test

**MAXIMUM LEGAL PERMISSIBLE
STRENGTH FOR FORWARD PROGRESS**

What?

**NO RIGHT TURN. RIGHT
LANE MUST TURN RIGHT**

So, the Left lane goes where?

**RIGHT LANE CLOSED FOR
NO APPARENT REASON**

A little honesty always appreciated.

ENTRANCE ONLY DO NOT ENTER

Is this like going Up the Down?

**NOT A THROUGH STREET
EVACUATION ROUTE**

Passage permissible in catastrophic events?

CAUTION WATER ON ROAD DURING RAIN

Road dry when sun shines?

ROAD UNSAFE WHEN UNDERWATER

Except for submarines and scuba divers, right?

**THE BRIDGE WILL BE CLOSED FOR
1 DAY BETWEEN OCT 17 AND 28**

Ladies and Gentlemen, place your bets!

**YOUR GPS IS WRONG. ROAD
CLOSED IN WINTER MONTHS
NO THROUGH TRAFFIC**

Recalculating. Pull out those paper maps.

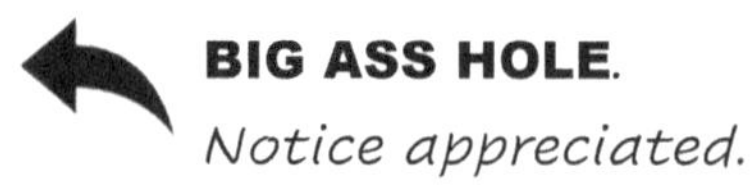 **BIG ASS HOLE**.

Notice appreciated.

USE CAUTION

POTHOLES, SINKHOLES,

ASSHOLES EVERYWHERE

Best Heads-Up Ever!

GO AHEAD DRINK AND DRIVE

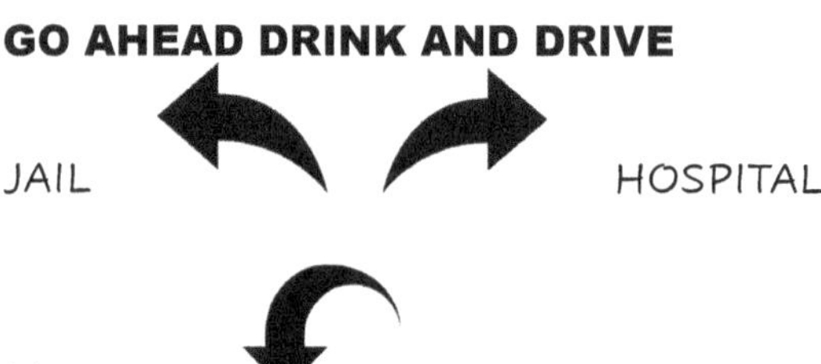

That about covers it.

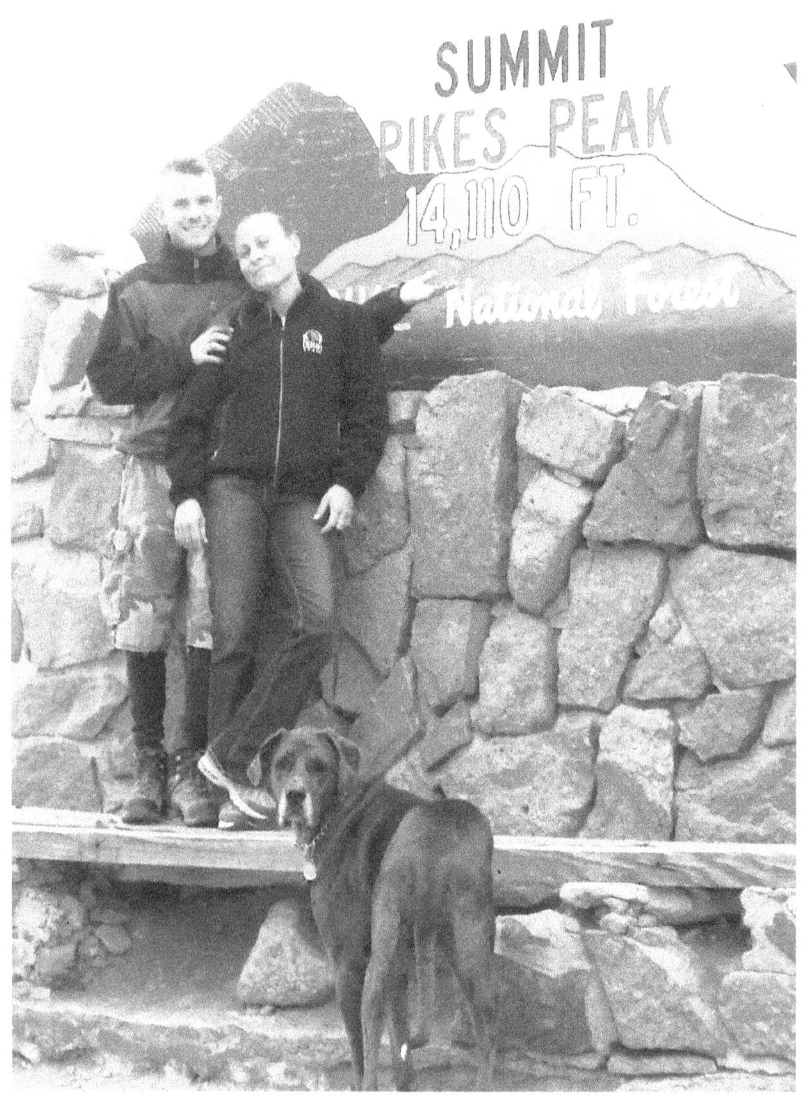

Victory

Victory

Stepping on to the planet's highest
tier is knowing the truth inside …
Joy comes not from the summit itself,
but rather from the struggle to attain.

Without valleys and crevasses, a flat
horizon devoid of peaks poses no challenges
yet to come. Every step is the prize already
in your grasp. Victory lies in the climb.

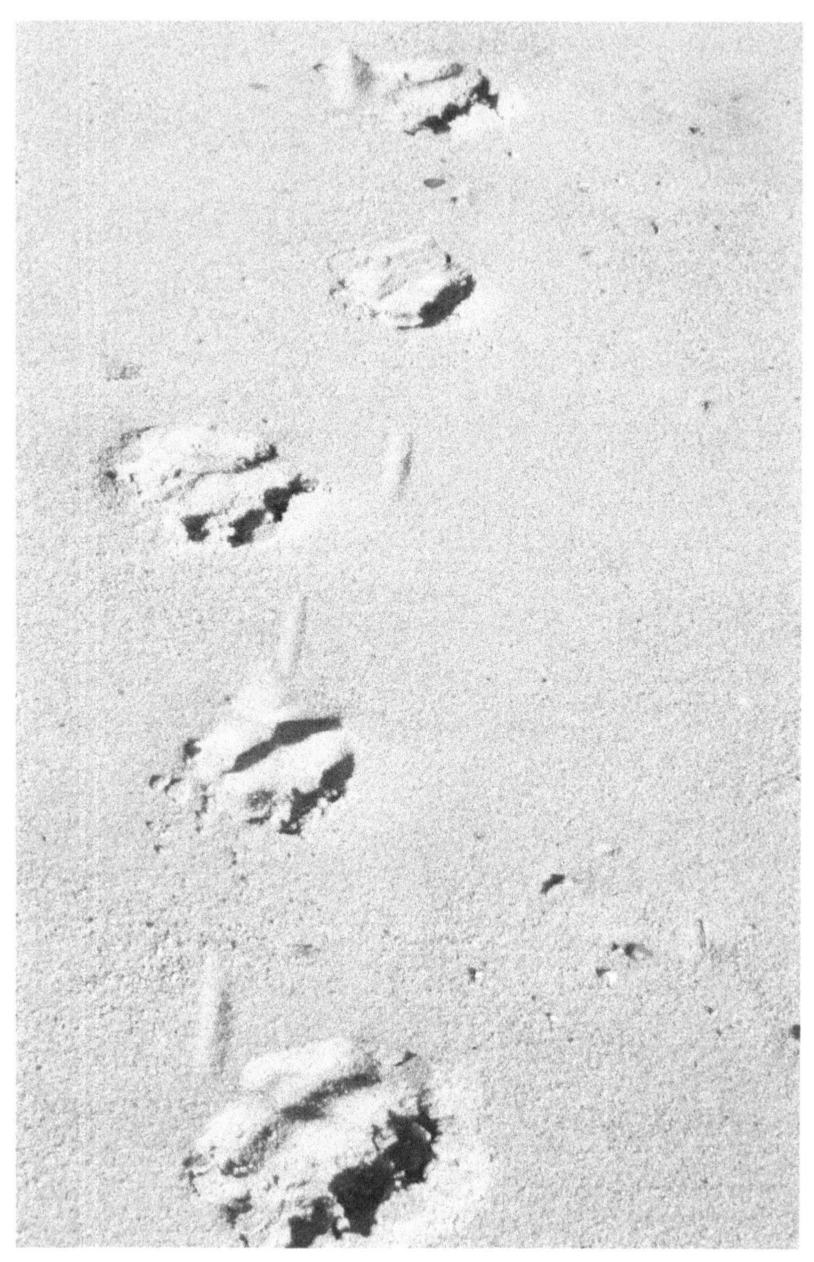

Walkin'

Walkin'

We went for a walk last night,
Sam, Dawg, and me.
Sam is the dog. Dawg is the cat.
Who would have thought we'd be three?

Dawg's our leader—
one bow-legged cat.
I keep pace in the middle;
Sam meanders up and back.

Can't say that I like this.
Oh, no, it's not fine.
This trio: me plus them
is not my design.

We don't belong to each other;
we just blunder along.
Dawg don't cotton to Sam.
Sam don't cotton to Dawg.

So, why this nightly ritual,
what's in it for we three?
Guess we're not particular
Sam, Dawg, and Me.

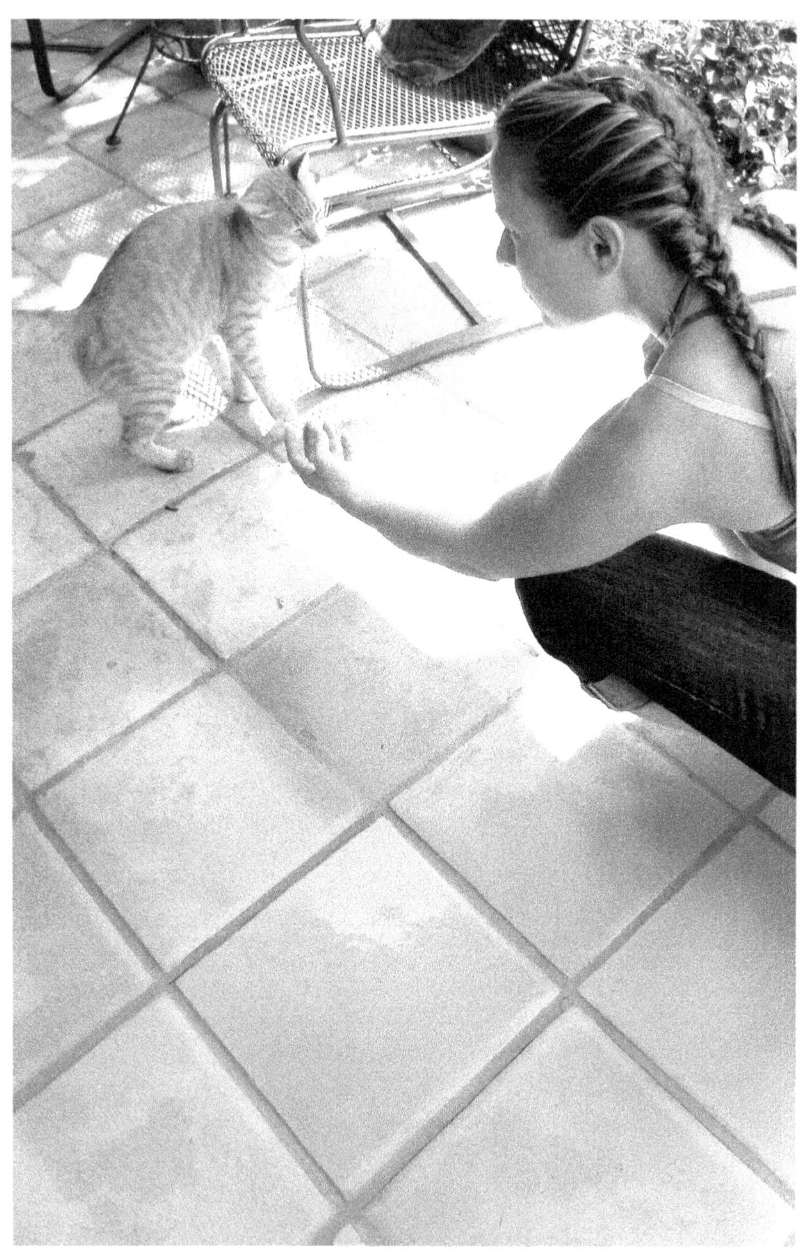

Sir Elton Non

Sir Elton Non

Sweet Nonny, you arrived with Dawg one day,
and decided the patio was the place to stay.
Battered and beaten, a scar on your face,
stitches, shots, then back to your space.

Dubbed Anonymous, unsure of the cat you'd be
a promise for a better name: we'll see, we'll see.
Together we made progress as you ate at my feet,
a grudging purr, feasting on treats.

Now you are Nonny, but ahead a long trail,
for my house, and your beloved patio were for sale.
Tinkerbell came, you put on your best show.
and it was off to Denver, flying high you'd go.

Dearest Nonny what a lucky cat you were to be
adopted by Tinkerbell, the best Mommy you see.
She let you be, creeping from feral to top cat,
a definite keeper. Who knew you'd be that?

On Patrick, your magic you worked—
a cat lover he was not,
yet despite misgivings knighted you were
Sir Elton Non. Lap time soon a favorite spot.

For nearly twenty years you'd been their fur baby,
loved and cherished despite vocals a tad high—just
maybe, a wee maybe. Sweet Nonny, Sir Elton Non etched
in their hearts, a nobler cat there was not.

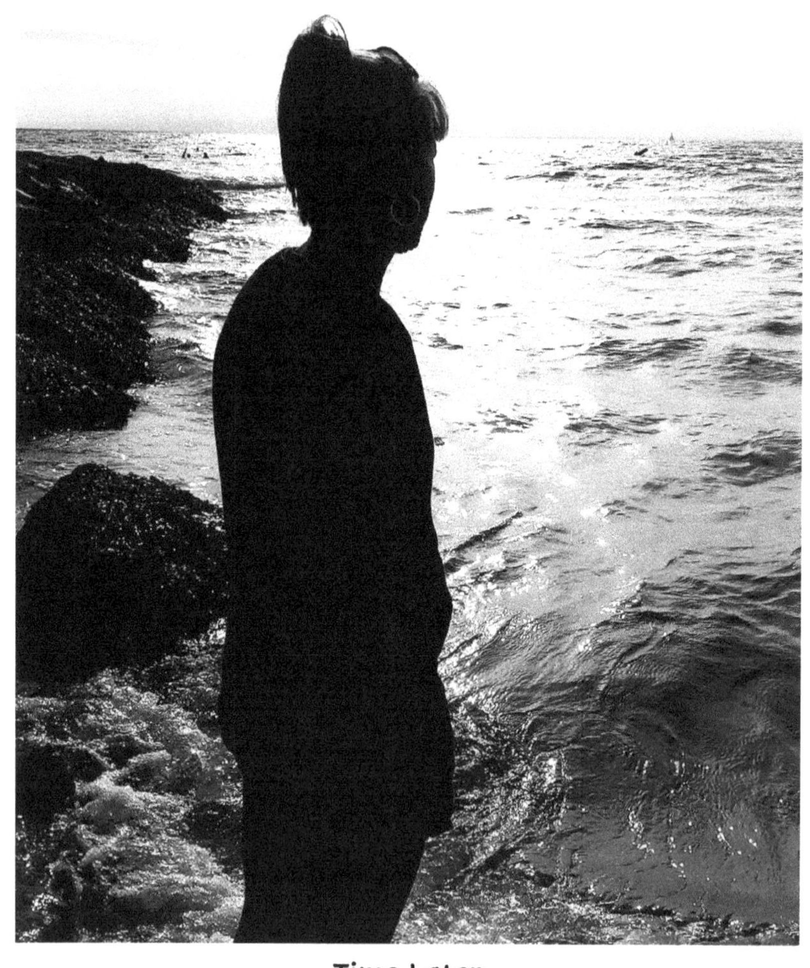

Time Later

Time Later

Can I tell you about that night the
tide gently unfurling, uncurling ....
Can I tell you, are you listening?

The night was soft, softly quiet ....
Your eyes they stray.
Are you with me still?

Time later to stop and stare,
say you scurrying on.

Time when?
It's late, you claim.
Too late? I ask.
Time later is your refrain.

Time Later? Tell me my friend,
where this place abounds?
Is it really within our grasp or
is it but a poor pacifier for
befuddled, muddled minds.

TIME NOW
CUE LIGHTS: Enter stage right.

TIME LATER
DIM LIGHTS: Exit stage left.
END SCENE: Close Curtains.

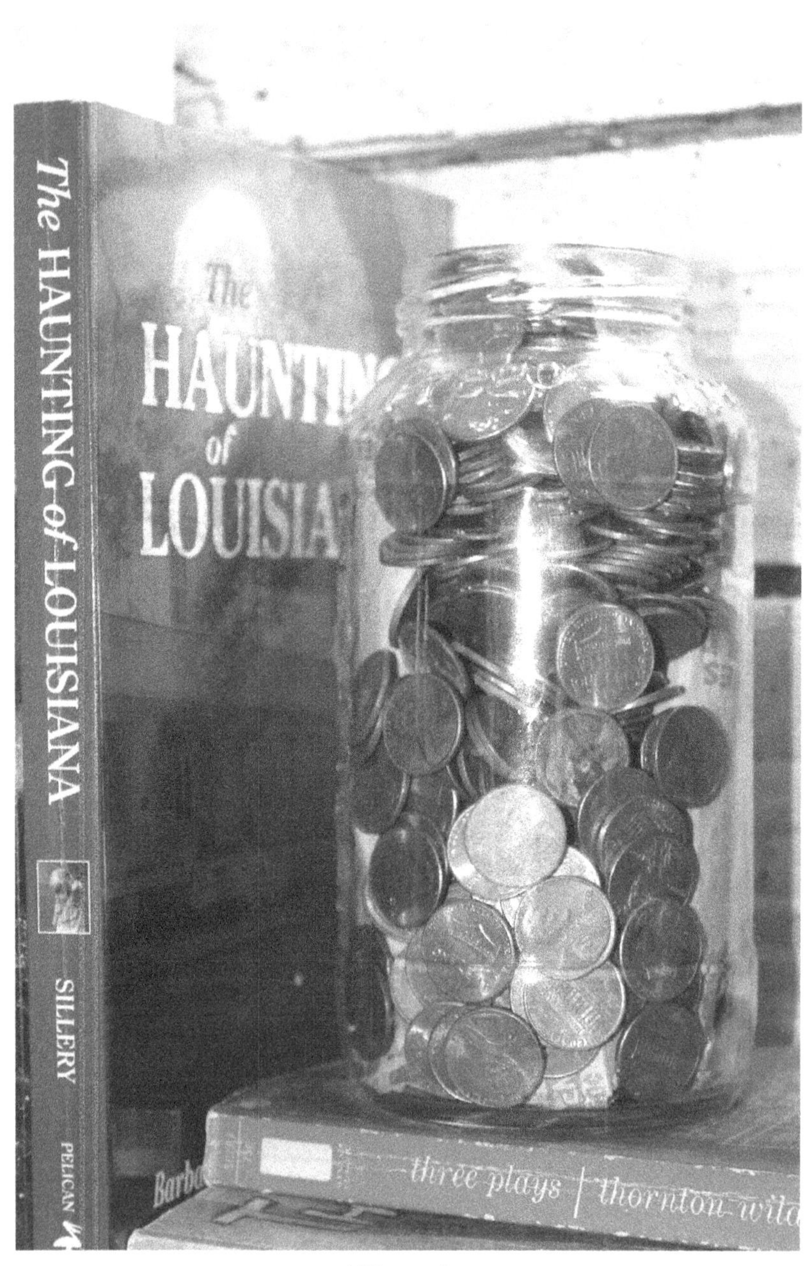

Killing Time

Killing Time

These are my moments,
coagulating like discarded
pennies stuck together in
a jelly jar prison, never to
be spent, never to function
as the currency of the realm,
doomed for eternity, copper
specks on the road to nowhere.

I passively sit doing nothing.
Is that still something? No tick.
No tock. No pendulum swing.
Killing time in a killing field.
Death by inertia.

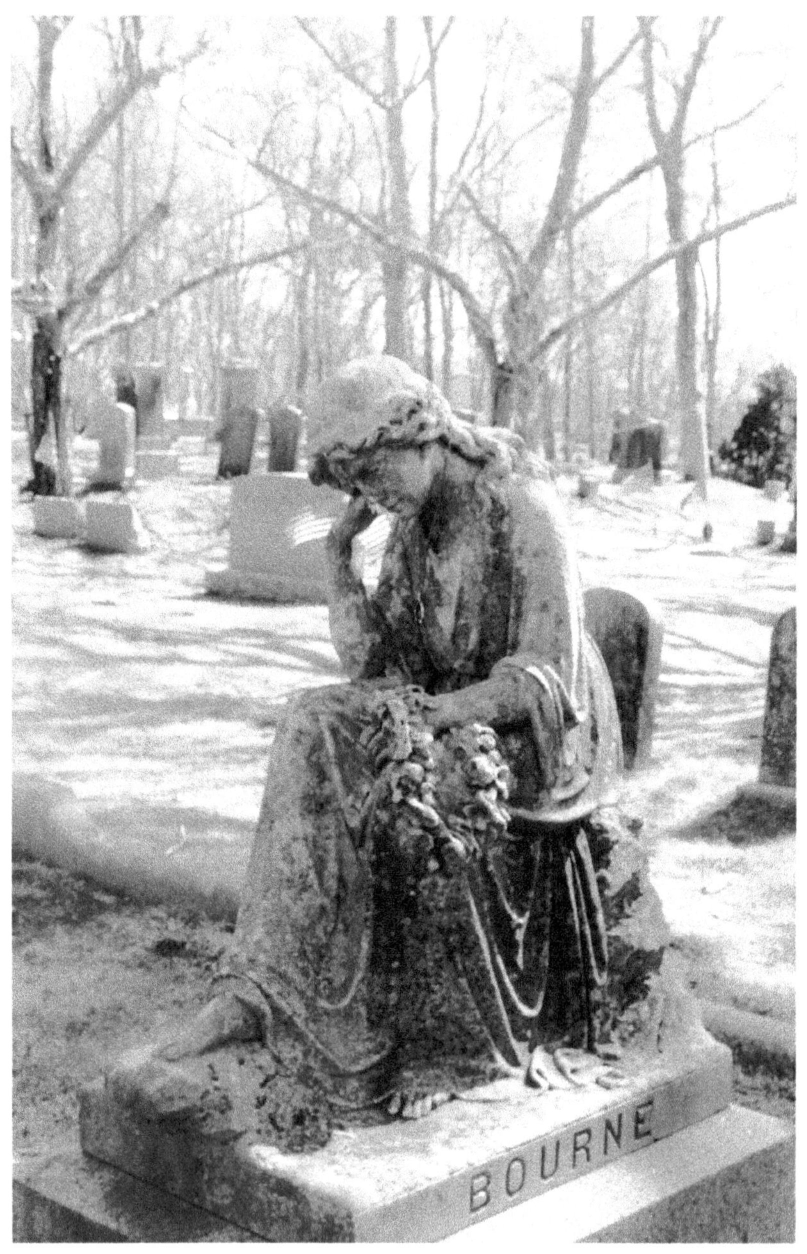

Que

Que

What is it, this moment, this uneasy kernel,
this fissure snaking up my spine? The coil
of my distorted thoughts binds me, unable
to unravel, detangle, wipe away this web.

One step forward, two steps back? No, I
will not do the dance. I will not play "What
does not kill you makes you stronger." I will
not pursue that existential ying and yang—
with no relief for my fermenting unease.

If philosophical diatribes follow the foot-
weary path, slipping down a fathomless
hole, then fellow travelers heed the call
of Chicken Little and run, run ....

The sky is falling.
              The sky is falling.

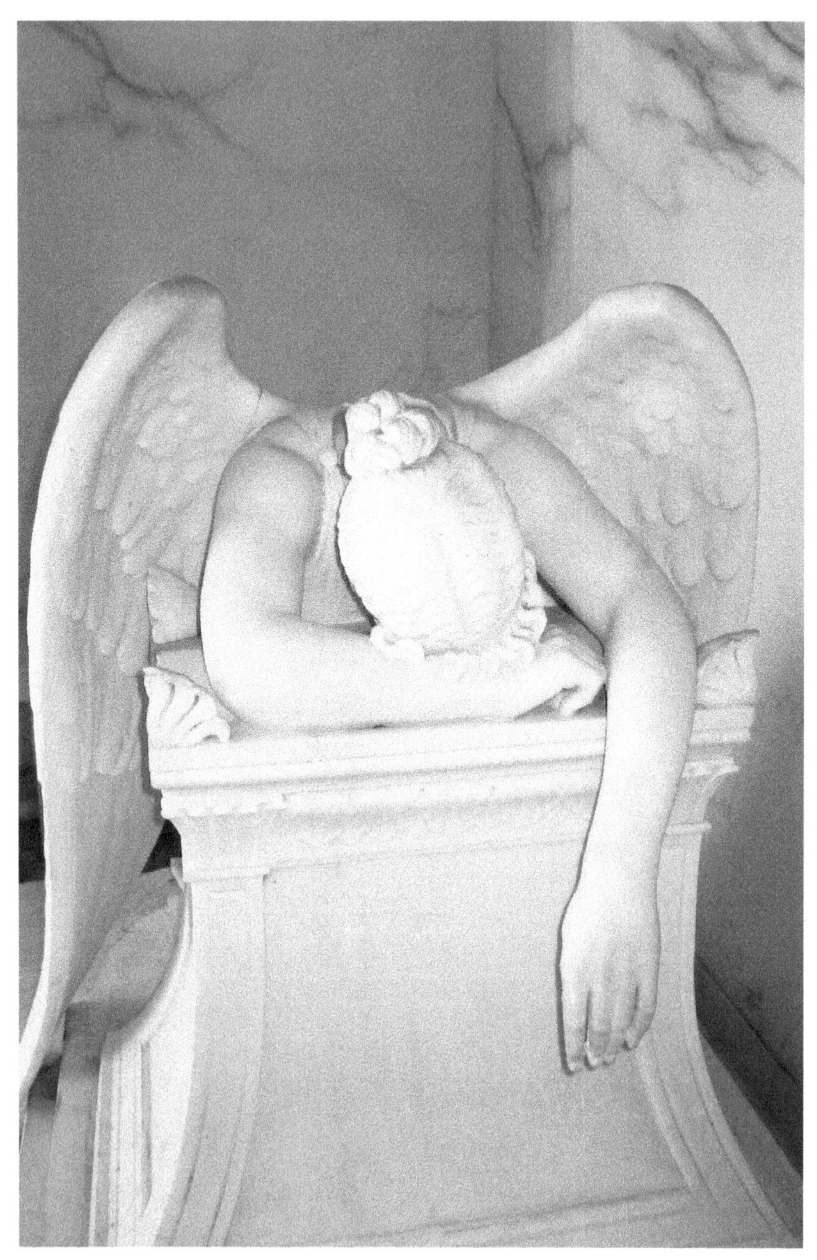

Not Today

Not Today

Fear is my reality, a bleak, black hole,
an endless loop. Groundhog Day minus
a return to the start.

I surrender to a life heavy with remorse,
recriminations, regrets, self-imposed
guilt, grief weary.

Carrying the burden of the past, slogging
through the present. Resigned. A martyr
to no cause.

Check and checkmate. Penultimate fate:
One day I will die—
just not today.

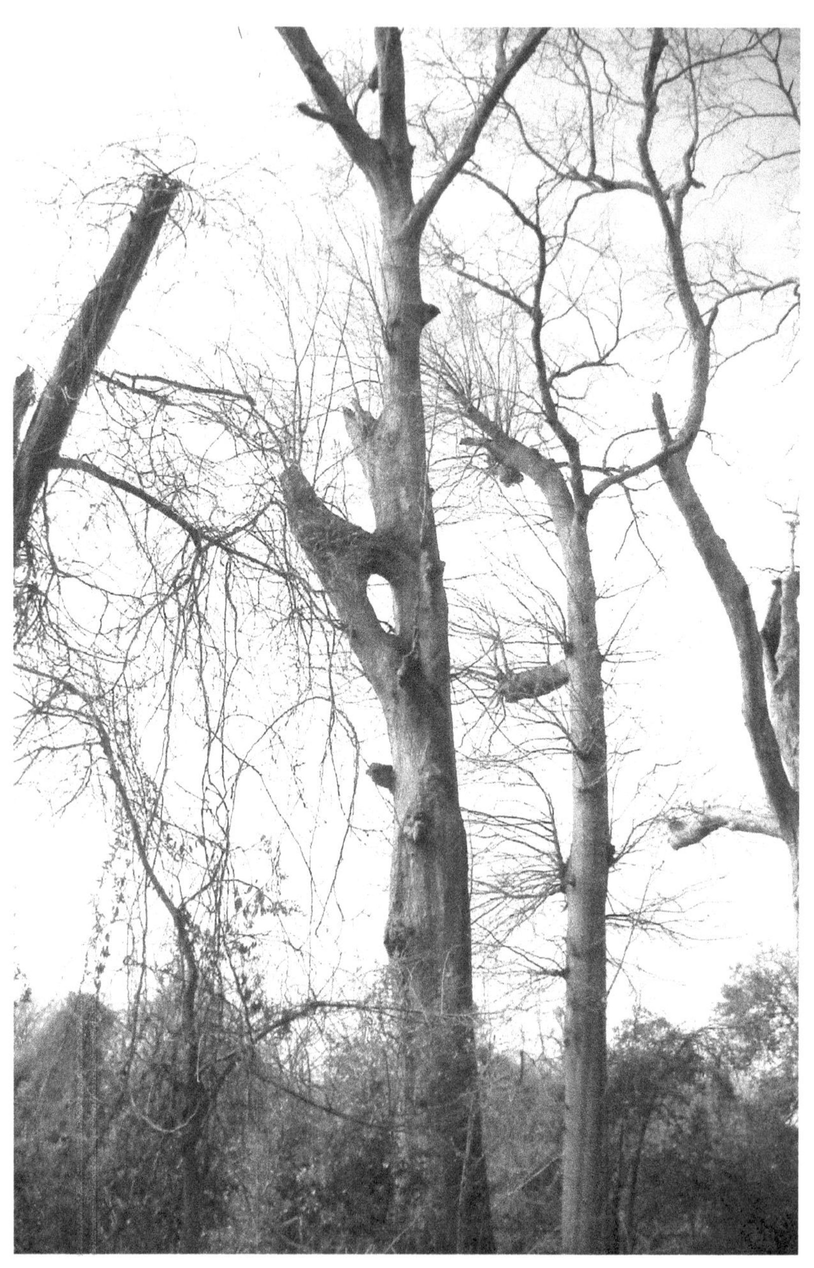

Attack of the Uglies

Attack of the Uglies

Dark, demented demons swooped down today—
a horde of feral beasts sucking air, blocking light,
pounding wings, piercing talons, choking out reason.

      UGLY

           UGLY

                UGLY

I flailed. I failed, lost another depressing round, but
who's counting? What's one battle between foes?

      Survivor Post-It Note:

      I'M STILL HERE.

      Why doesn't it feel that way?

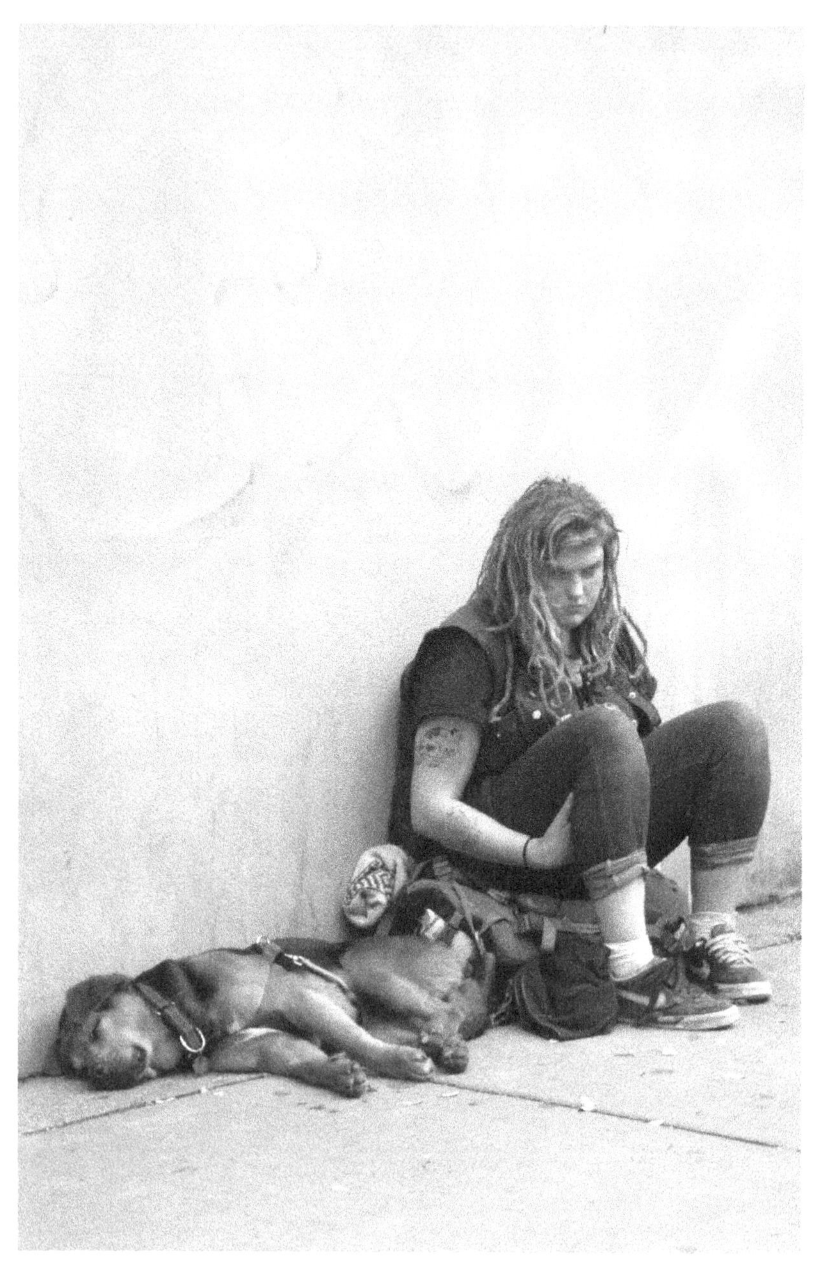

Fixin' to ...

Fixin' to ...

My Anger.
        My Hurt.
                My Pain.
                        My Past.

It validates me.
MOVE ON!

It's killing me.
        LET IT GO!

                    FIXIN' TO . . .

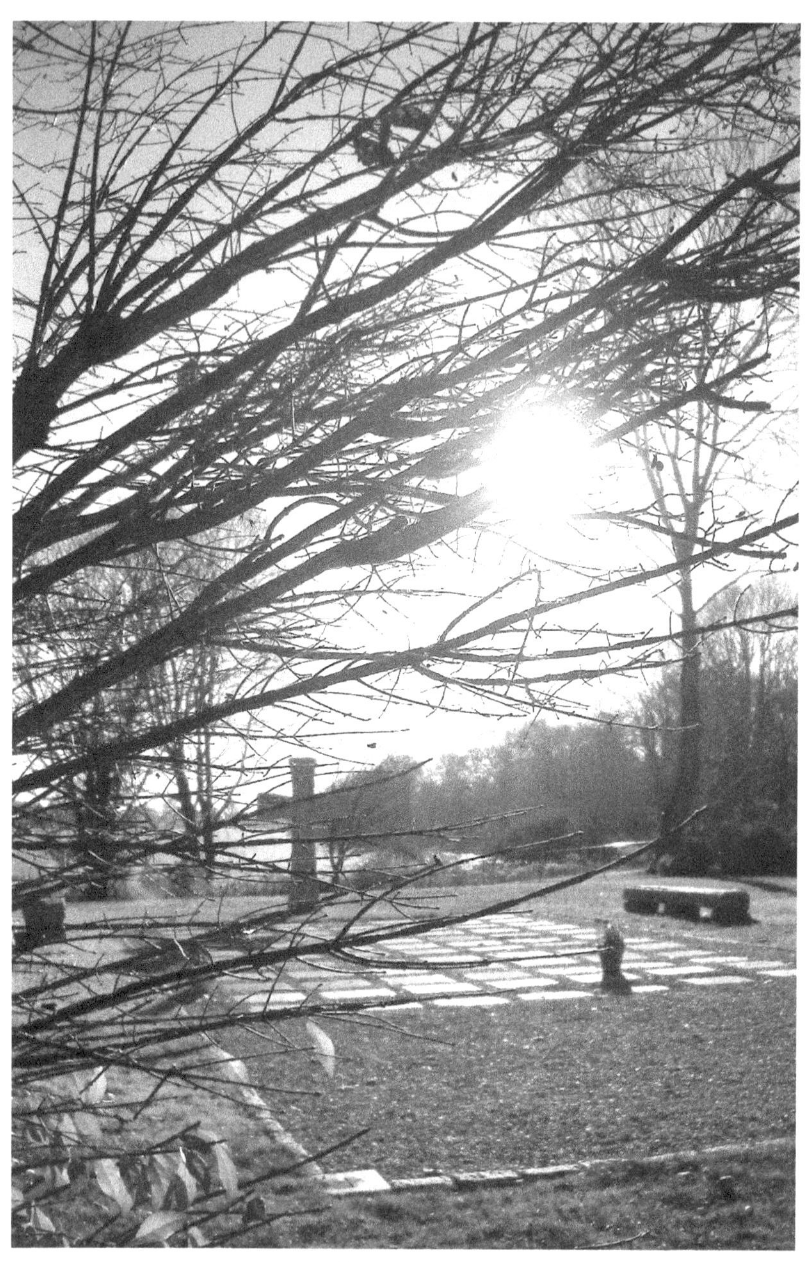

Another One Down

Another One Down

Hello, Death.
You're back. Again.

No warning,
        unwanted,
                uninvited,
                        barging brazenly in.

Without the blanket of family,
however worn and torn, captive in
grief, the solitary world engulfs me.

Devoid of shared recollections—
no longer daughter, sister, lost in
the labyrinth, mine now to process
alone.

Wandering, unearthing forgotten
family lore, digging up this and that,
missing the comforting echoes of
Remember when?

My friend revels in being an elder
of his tribe, an honor earned.
I must learn to do the same.

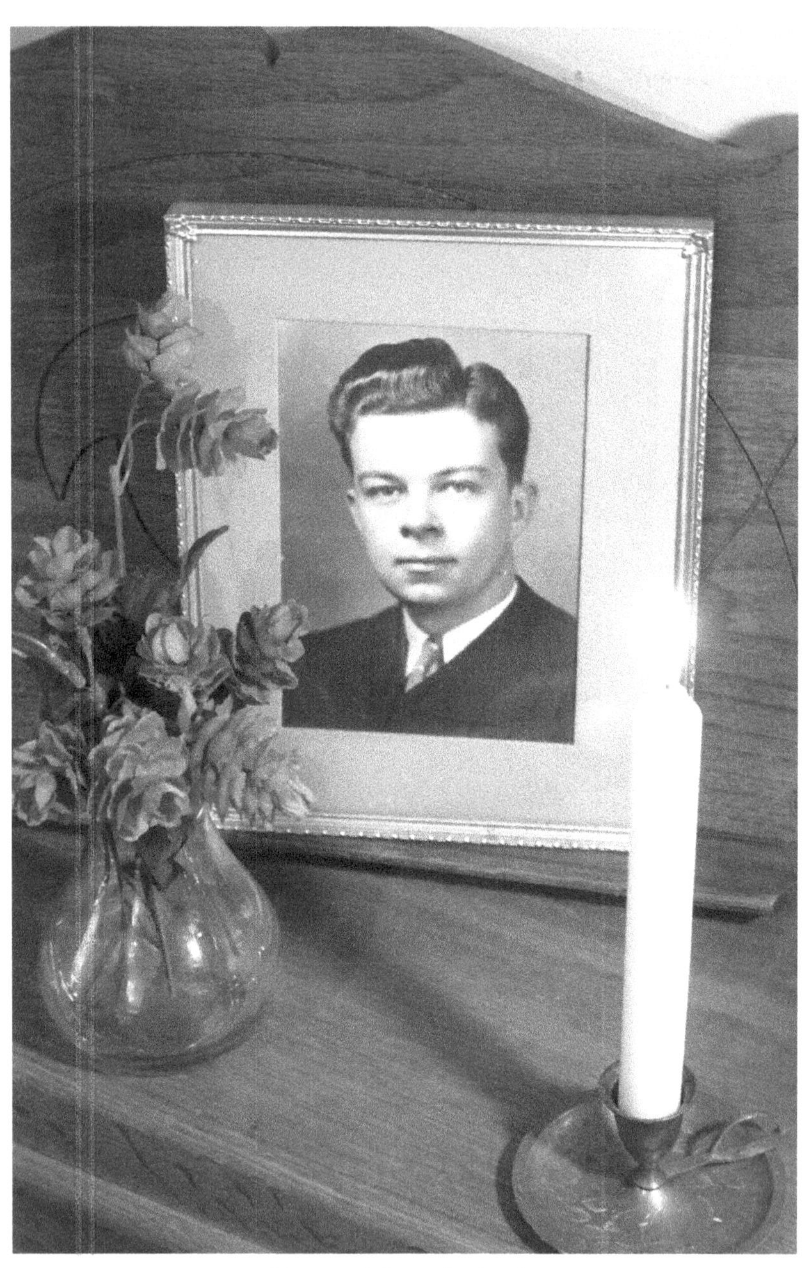

Man with Suit & Tie

Man with Suit & Tie

At the open coffin spectacle, mourners shuffle like
art gallery aficionados, forming an eerie parade.
On exhibit not the masterful classic—Vermeer's
Girl with a Pearl Earring–but rather a misguided
mockery: *Man with Suit and Tie.*

Dressed and stuffed, smile locked in a grimace,
dazzling blue eyes pinned shut, tie tightly
knotted round the throat. Where is the
humanity in such a haunting portrayal?

The wax effigy does not make him
     any
          less
               dead.

Hear him mourners as he silently shouts:

    Close the lid and let me be.
    I no longer am.

Oh, to erase the burning image of that travesty,
and treasure instead the memory of a vibrant
man, who gave so much to me.

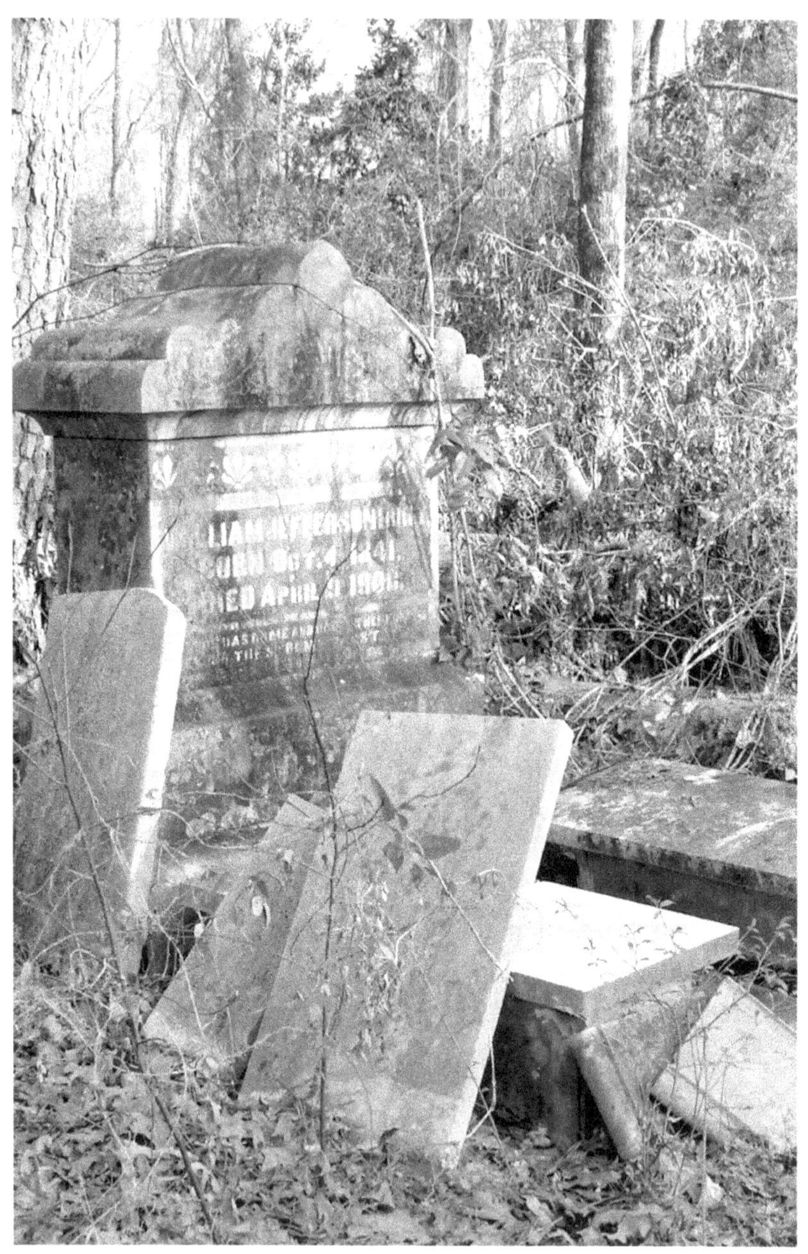

Gone

Gone

Conjugate the basics:
He's dead.
She's dead.
They're dead.

Eliminate the euphemisms,
phase out the platitudes,
banalities, bromides:
Passed
Passed over
Passed away,
Crossed the Bar
In a Better Place
Met Their Maker
And by all means,
RIP, Rest in Peace.

Less eloquent, but just as ambiguous
the dearly departed have:
Kicked the Bucket
Bought the Farm
Bit the Dust
Gave up the Ghost
Lost the Battle
Checked out and
are now Six Feet Under.

GONE, remains the ultimate non-committal
version of the status quo. GONE, four letters
like DEAD, but lacking that finality, trailing a
faint hope that a return might be imminent.

Minus plans to prop the deceased up in the
coffin, pass death off as a momentary blip
in the circle of life, why the proliferation
of deceptive, disingenuous, misleading,
misguided, misinformation?

Do cliches hold grief at bay? Soften the blow?
Dead: not alive. No coming back. No regeneration.
One word. Four letters. D-E-A-D.

In the immortal words of Bugs Bunny:

That's All, Folks!

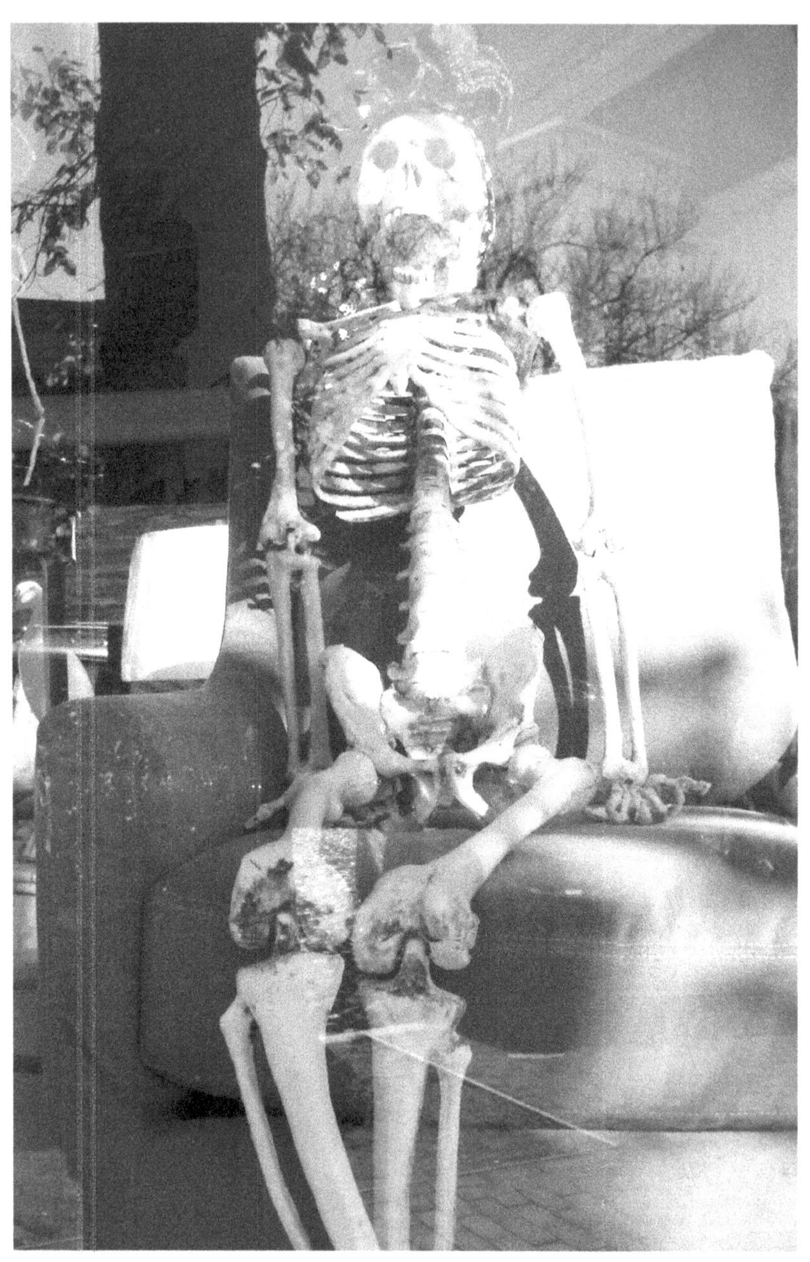

Kiss My Grits

Kiss My Grits

Notes on mourning southern style:

When I inevitably cease to be,
Kiss my grits, honey,
and set me free.

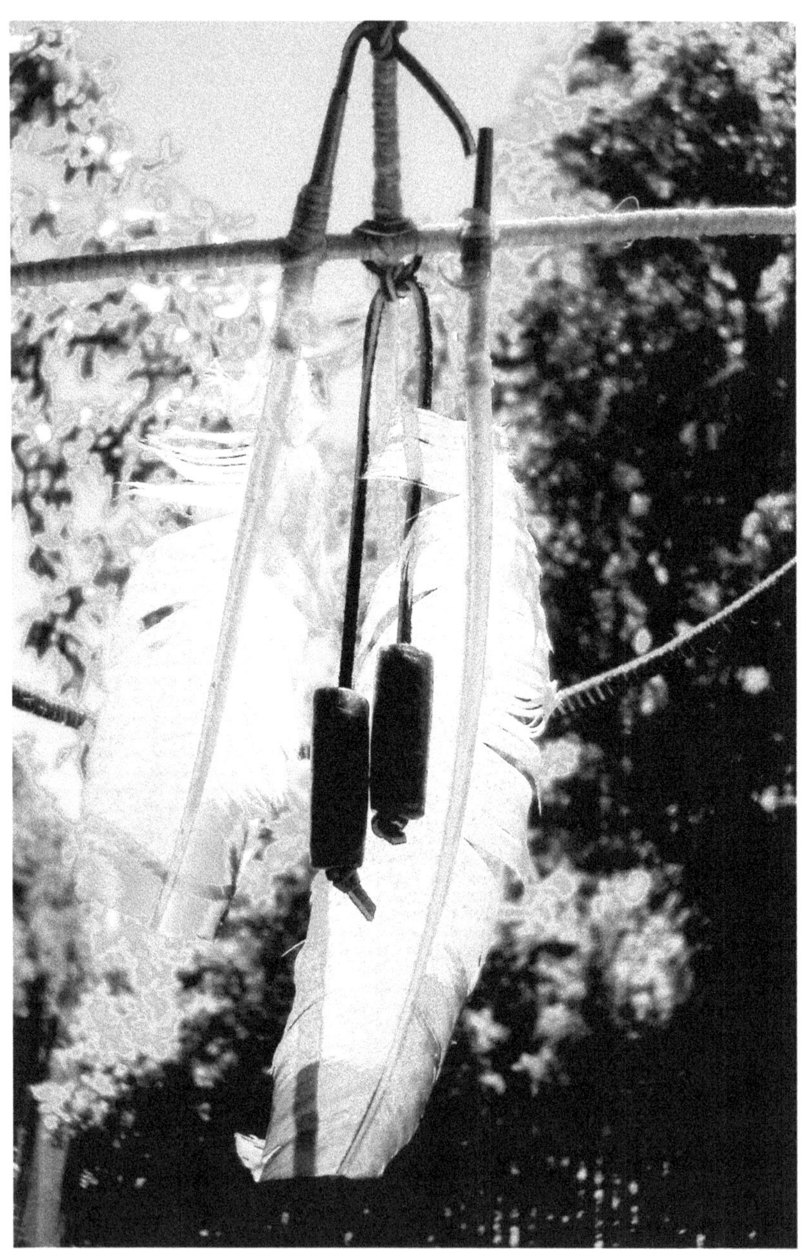

The Old Ways Live

The Old Ways Live

Iti Houma
traiteur and traiteuse,
calumets and crawfish,
palmetto huts and pirogues.
Calling of the Tribes, Pow Wows,
drumming circles, Intertribals, men's
fancy, women's shawl and jingle dances.
Spanish moss dolls and half-hitch coil baskets.
Bayous Chene, Dularge, Dulac, Ile à Jean Charles,
Grand Bois, LaFourche, Houma, and Golden Meadow.

The old ways live.
Despite migrations, tragedies,
assimilation, abandoned settlements, hearts,
hands, minds prevail—a journey of skills mastered,
traditions honored. Respected Houma elders, cultural
forebearers: Rosalie Courteau, Hazel Lombas, Marie Dean
Morning Dove, Joe Dardard, Janie Verret Luster, Grayhawk. A
continuum, sharing, reaching into the future, keeping the past
alive An Irrevocable obligation to the people and the
earth, preserved for those that follow, enriching us all.

I am humbled by lessons learned.
Yakuke (Thank you)

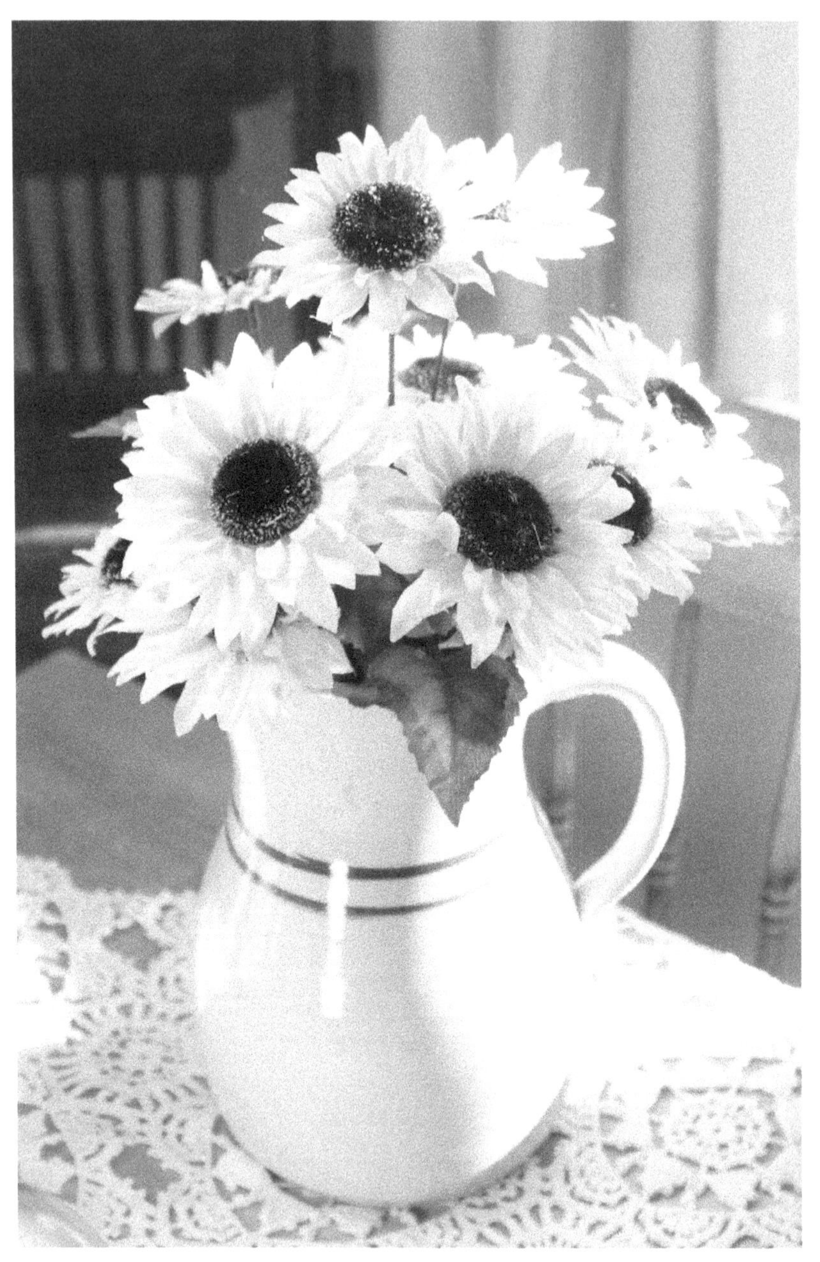

I Didn't Ask

I Didn't Ask

I didn't ask why you left your beloved
country. Hopeful? Determined?
Desperate?

I didn't ask why a skilled cabinetmaker
abandoned his craft to begin again in a
strange new world.

I didn't ask why a young wife, clutching
a toddler, anxiously waited, counting the
days until her husband could save them.

I didn't ask how a man scrimped and saved
till his arms once again embraced the family
his heart held dear.

I didn't ask how a "mere" housewife
hoarded money in secret caches under
rugs to proudly purchase a first home.

I never asked or tried to speak your
native tongue. I remained ignorant of
the words that flowed.

I knew you only as tiny, wizened gnomes, not
a loving couple who rebuilt their lives, so their
daughters and sons could live as Americans.

I did not know. I did not ask.
Forgive my youth. Forgive my lack
of pride in my heritage.

Dear grandparents, only now,
decades later, do I stand steadfast
behind Ukraine.

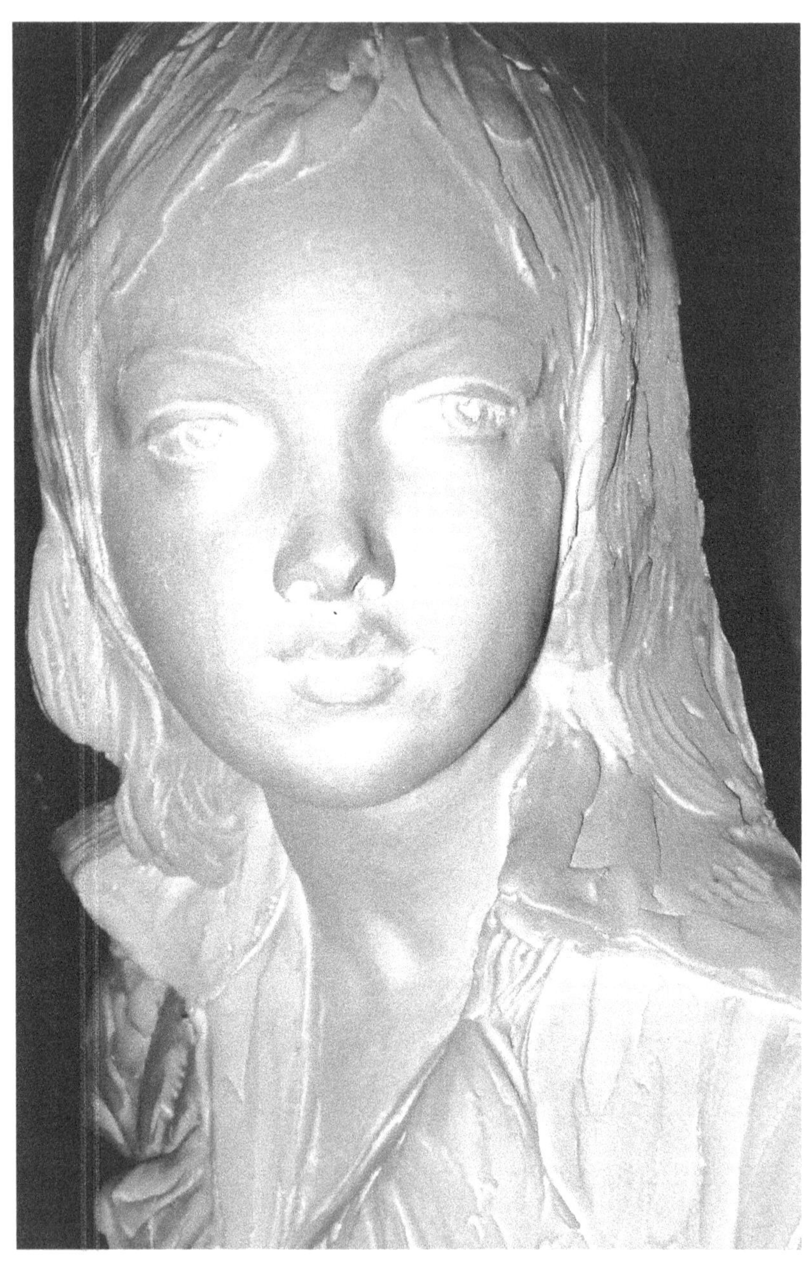

Ghosts Within

Ghosts Within

Ghosts without and ghosts within
haunt the hollows of our souls. It's
not the dead we need to fear, it's the
living ghastly ghouls.

Let the spirits succor, a comforting
presence be, for they live on through
love, echoes of once was, now free.

Cleanse tormented thoughts. Release
worrying regrets. Breathe deeply, allow
nature to share her heart hugs. Weave
a new path. Life is yours to embrace.

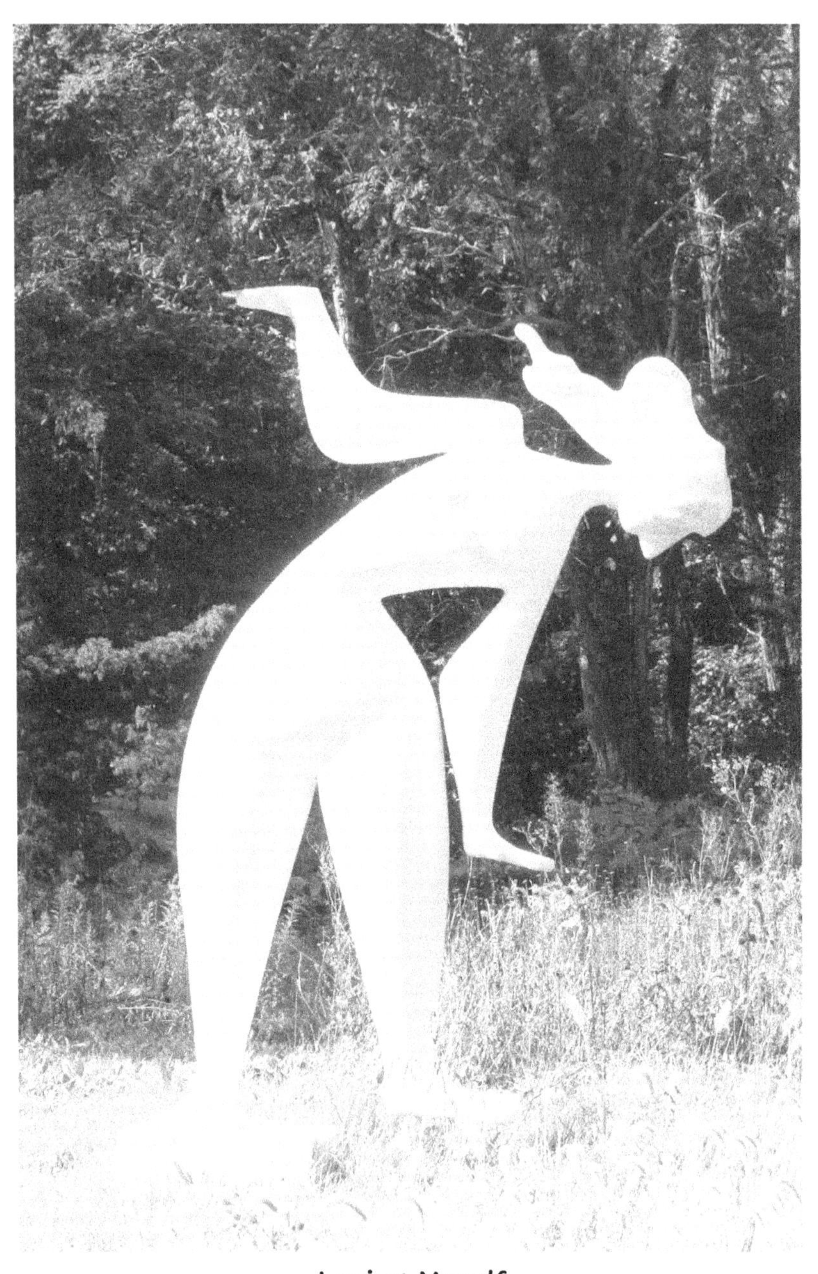

Loving Myself
Sculptor Thomas Maley. Bad Martha Brewery,
Falmouth, MA.

Loving Myself

I live alone, work alone,
navigate solo at the beach,
attend parties minus a plus one.
Is loving myself enough?

If I pat my talented self on the
back for every goal achieved, do
I need others to validate me?
Is loving myself enough?

If family, friends, colleagues offer a
hug, a nod of encouragement, in Creole
Louisiana, that's lagniappe, a wonderful
extra bonus.
Is loving myself enough?

Now, long past the halfway mark,
reflecting on where I've been—battles
won and lost, I smile, for I know now that ...

Loving myself is enough.

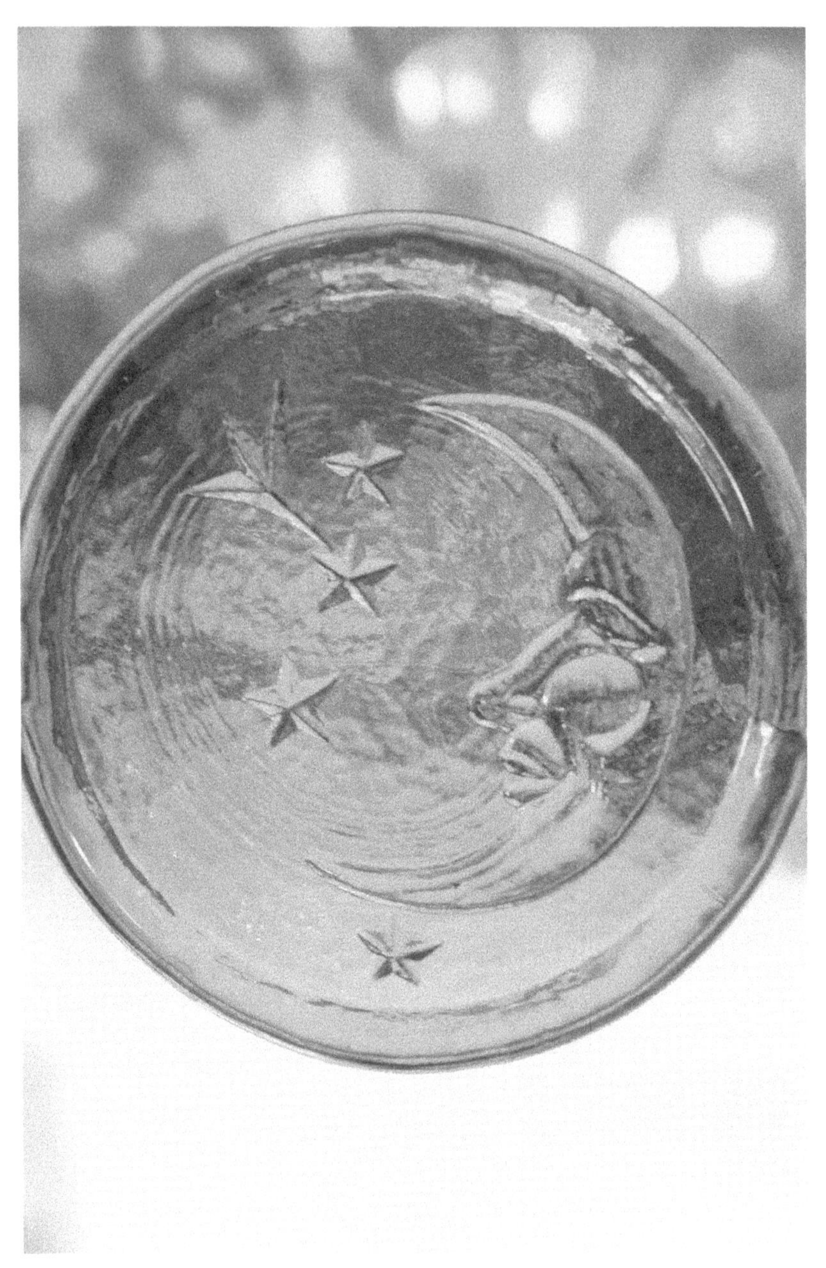

Thank you, Sir James M. Barrie

Thank you, Sir James M. Barrie

There it is Wendy! Second star to the
right and straight on 'til morning.

If Peter Pan and Tinkerbell can navigate
their way home by turning right at the
next star, and sailors plot their course by
looking up, then there is hope for the rest
of us plodding
          through
                    the dark.

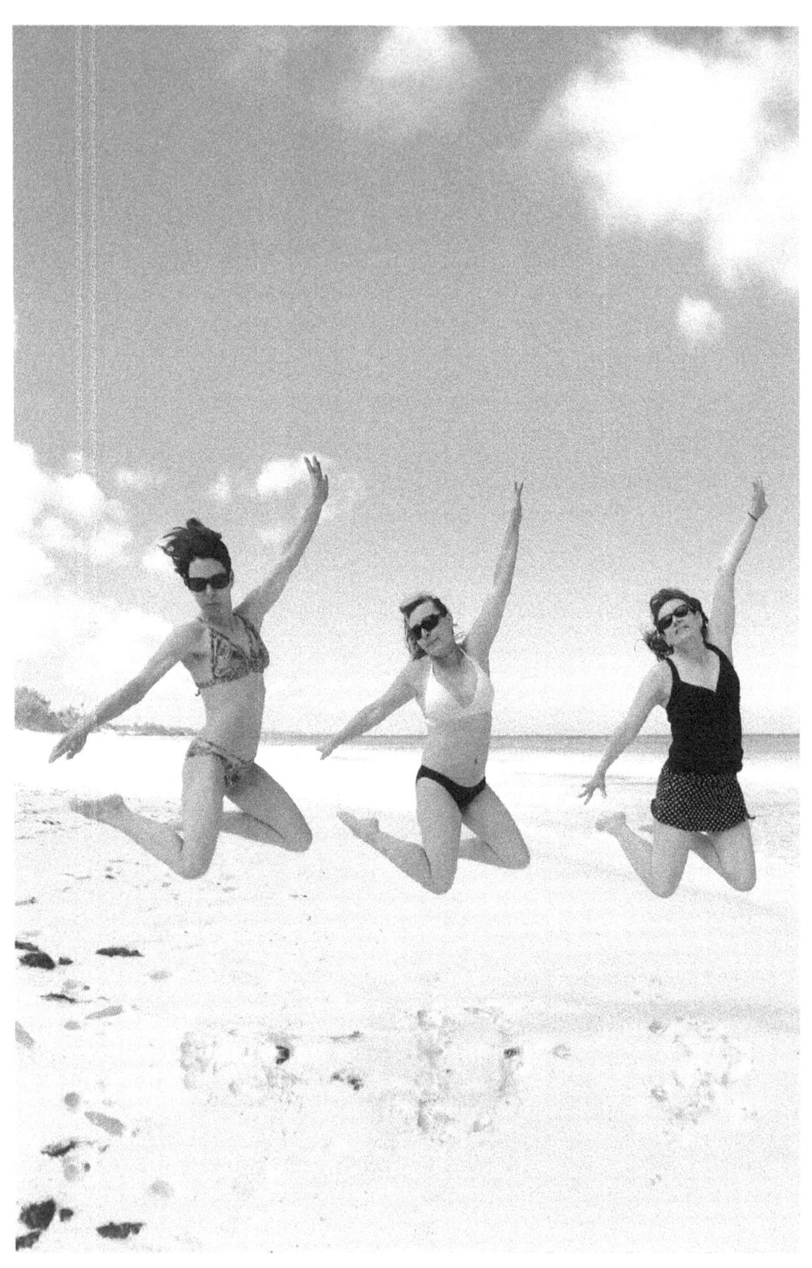

Do That
Photo by Patrick Eul

What soothes your soul ...

—DO THAT

Acknowledgements

During the course of my career, I have written for a diverse range of formats: television, print, podcasts, radio, trade show news and even liner notes for CDs. I have covered a wide assortment of topics: wooden boats, a native American tribal group, Creole planation architecture, numerous ghosts and their antics, along with planes, cars, trucks, amusement parks, analytical chemistry and applied spectroscopy, porta potties and the proverbial kitchen sink.

I have always admired poets and their amazing ability to tell a story and touch the heart with a few perfect words. This time around I challenged myself to tackle a new literary format to hopefully share some of life's joys and foibles.

I would not be who I am today without the love and support of my daughters, Danielle, Rebecca, and Heather (Tinkerbell). Having a best friend is a wonderful bonus, as they say in Creole Louisiana, that's lagniappe. Thank you, Glinda, for all you do.

The images as they appear in this book would not have been possible without the talents of my son-in-law, graphic designer and photo editor Patrick Eul. Patrick transformed my images into art along with designing the cover. I am forever grateful.

Thank you to everyone at Pen Women Press, especially Lucy Arnold, Art Editor and Publications chair.

To all those who have read my books and watched my television shows and features, thank you. For those who have come to my book talks and presentations, thank you. As writers, we often work in solitude and are enormously grateful for your feedback. I do my best to answer emails.

I leave you with the immortal words of Dr. Suess: *"Don't cry because it's over, smile because it happened!"* I smile everyday for the wonderful people in my life.

Thank you all

Barbara

About the Author

Barbara Sillery is an award-winning television producer and script writer. Sillery is also the author of nine books of haunted folklore and legends. Her work has appeared in numerous anthologies and three of her books have been adapted for children. As the former president and owner of Lagniappe Media, her company specialized in cultural 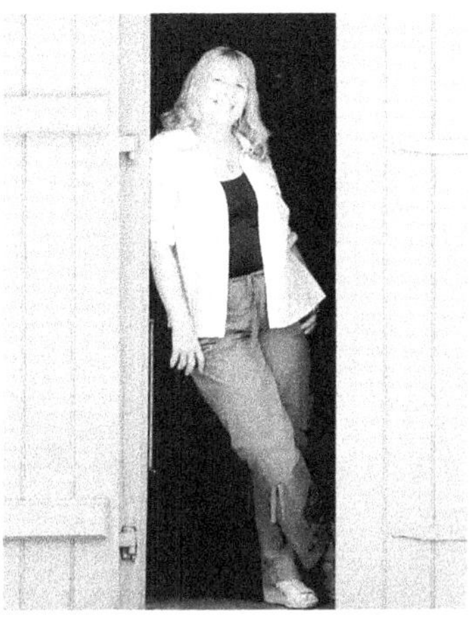 documentaries broadcast on PBS affiliates around the country. She served as a Field Producer for syndicated television shows: *Extra,* the *Travel Channel, Strange Universe, Celebrity Justice, CBS News,* and the *Early* show. Sillery has also contributed articles to *Native Peoples, La Vie,* and *Louisiana Life* magazines. Her accolades include the International Worldfest Awards, several Tellys, Women in Communication, and New Orleans Press Club awards, along with recognition form PBS and the American Association for State and Local History. Born on a United States Air Force Base, she grew up in New York, attended university in Pennsylvania, and raised her three daughters in New Orleans. She now resides on Cape Cod where she continues to write and produce videos for regional museums and non-profits. To find out more, please go to www.barbarasillery.com .

"Words are my passion, and the journey is awesome. I climbed a rickety ladder into the belvedere of an abandoned plantation house and gone down into the bowels of a rotting shrimp boat. I danced at pow wows and searched for headstones in a rural cemetery. I happily follow a tale wherever it takes me." —Barbara Sillery

"Barbara's gift for storytelling holds in the written word, just as it does for television."—Phillip J. Jones, former Secretary of Louisiana's Department of Culture, Recreation and Tourism

"Sillery is not merely a storyteller, but a historian as well."—Renee Peck, Columnist, New Orleans Times-Picayune.